Wicked Virginia City

Wicked Virginia City

Peter B. Mires

The History Press

Published by The History Press
Charleston, SC
www.historypress.com

First published 2020

Manufactured in the United States

ISBN 9781467144308

Library of Congress Control Number: 2020934361

This book is dedicated to Dan De Quille and Alf Doten.

CONTENTS

PREFACE

Virginia had grown to be the "livest" town, for its age and population, that America had ever produced. The sidewalks swarmed with people—to such an extent, indeed, that it was generally no easy matter to stem the human tide.... There were military companies, fire companies, brass bands, banks, hotels, theatres, "hurdy-gurdy houses," wide-open gambling palaces, political pow-wows, civic processions, street fights, murders, inquests, riots, a whisky mill every fifteen steps...a dozen breweries and half a dozen jails and station-houses in full operation, and some talk of building a church.

—Mark Twain

Virginia City, Nevada, has a rightful place in the lore and legend of the Old West. Mark Twain wrote about this mining boomtown in *Roughing It* (1872); it was the urban epicenter of the television show *Bonanza*; and Western genre writers, such as Louis L'Amour and Richard Wheeler, found Virginia City an ideal setting for their rootin' tootin' tales. It was the quintessential Wild West town, complete with saloons, prostitutes, gunfights, hangings and, as Twain noted with no small amount of sarcasm, some talk of building a church.

Some of the Wild West aspects attributed to Virginia City are myths. The town actually contained several fine churches, and not every woman was a prostitute and not every man a gunslinger. On the other hand, there is much about this Wild West town that is based on fact. For instance, the public hanging execution of the man accused of murdering a popular prostitute attracted an estimated crowd of four thousand that included women,

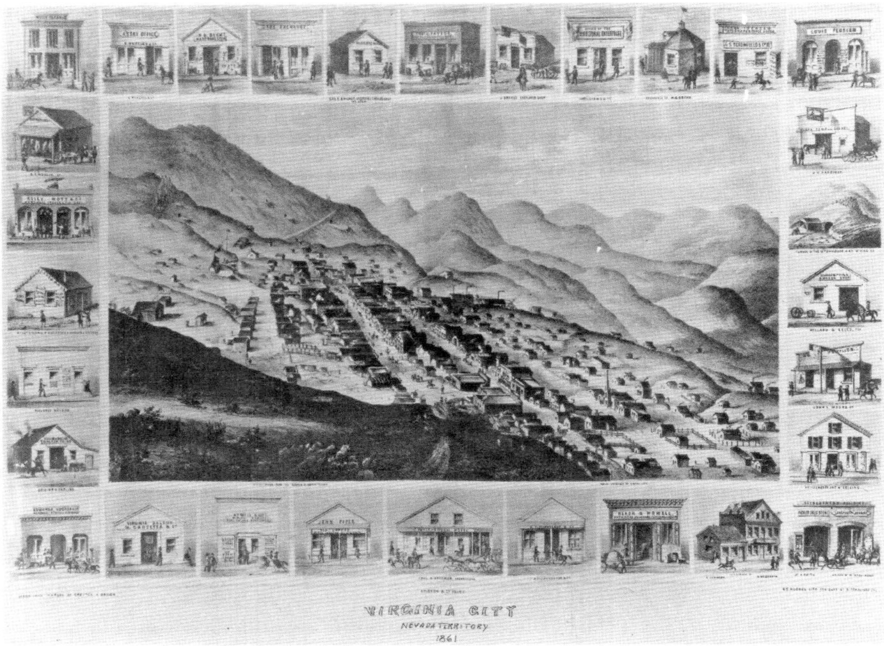

Virginia City, Nevada Territory, 1861. *Drawing by Grafton T. Brown. Courtesy of the Special Collections Department, University of Nevada–Reno Libraries.*

children and picnic baskets—this is the stuff of The History Press's Wicked Series and, therefore, the focus of this book.

One could argue that the character of the present-day state of Nevada originated with this frontier boomtown. Nevada is the only state in which prostitution is legal; Reno and Las Vegas remain icons of casino gambling; slot machines are ubiquitous; and there are no blue laws restricting the sale of alcohol. Nevadans, however, are no more wicked than any other citizens of this country; it is just that they abhor any attempt to legislate morality—a legacy they inherited from Virginia City.

As tempting as it is to trace a trajectory from the boomtown of Virginia City to the present, this book does not pertain to modern Nevada. Its coverage is limited to a period bracketed between the 1850s and the 1880s, with most of the narrative taking place between 1859, when the Comstock Lode was discovered, and 1879, when the mining boom called the Big Bonanza ended.

During those boom years, the mining frenzy of the Comstock Lode amassed more than $300 million in gold and silver, a figure that would be

J. Ross Browne illustration, "My Claim, Sir!" *Author's collection.*

expressed in billions today. A sizable percentage of that gold was discovered during the era known as the Big Bonanza, which occurred between 1873 and 1879. Fortunes came and went with the vagaries of lady luck or by calculated means and machinations, but money abounded, and Virginia City reveled in its newfound wealth.

Virginia City was the most prominent of several neighboring communities—including Gold Hill, Silver City and Dayton—that were directly involved in mining and milling ore from the Comstock Lode. Virginia City was the county seat of Storey County, which also included Gold Hill, and contained most of the county's peak population of twenty-five thousand in the Big Bonanza years.

In the first few years of its existence, Virginia City was a man's world. Men outnumbered women, and children were a rarity. In 1862, when the boomtown was only a few years old, men comprised 85 percent of the population. Even at the height of Virginia City's mining boom, the male-female ratio was seventy-thirty. As a generalization, women and families had an ameliorating influence on Virginia City's rowdy atmosphere, as they had

J. Ross Browne illustration, "Ladies of the Hotel." *Author's collection.*

among the bachelor society of California's Mother Lode. It was, relatively speaking, a tamer place in 1880 than it was in 1860.

Another characteristic of Virginia City was its ethnic diversity, which mirrored the international composition of those who participated in the California gold rush. A perusal of the U.S. decennial censuses for 1870 and 1880 or, better yet, a stroll through the Virginia City Cemetery, will testify to the diversity of the area's foreign immigrants. Most descended from northern and western Europe, with the Irish, Cornish (called "Cousin Jacks" in the mining West) and Germans comprising the three largest European ethnic groups.

One reality of the era, unfortunately, was the existence of discrimination. The Mexican-American War (1846–1848) was still fresh in the minds of many, and prejudices that existed against Mexicans in the California Mother Lode carried over to the Comstock. Tensions with the local Paiute Tribe culminated in the Pyramid Lake War of 1860, which left Native Americans as a marginalized minority. The Chinese in Virginia City lived a precarious existence as a stigmatized, yet tolerated, population. The small number of African Americans in the area fared a little better, perhaps because of the pro-Union sentiment in Virginia City during the American Civil War (1861–1865).

Regardless of their backgrounds and circumstances, people came to Virginia City for one reason: to make money. Some made an obscene amount of money; Irishman John Mackay arrived broke and became one of the wealthiest men in the world. He and his business partners, James Fair, James Flood and William O'Brien, were known to all as the "Bonanza Kings." Representing the Bank of California, William Sharon showed a talent—which some called an unscrupulous talent—for industrial monopoly and

Virginia City, looking northwest, circa 1878. *Courtesy of the Special Collections Department, University of Nevada–Reno Libraries.*

amassed a fortune as a result. Others who made their pile included "Lucky" Baldwin; "Sandy" and Eilley Bowers; Alvinza Hayward; and George Hearst. Some made money by "mining the miners." Comstock miners were unionized and among the best paid in the world for that vocation. They had money to spend, and Virginia City's one hundred saloons happily accommodated them, as did the city's working girls, card sharks, stock swindlers, robbers and a host of others—not all of them nefarious.

Virginia City lived up to, and indeed defined, our modern image of a mining boomtown. The thousands who came did not do so for the scenic beauty of the place; it was and is a sagebrush- and rock-strewn mountain slope. They came because there was money to be made—by hook or by crook. Virginia City quickly took on a veneer of sophistication, especially with its architectural gems, like the International Hotel, the Storey County Courthouse and "Millionaires Row," but it was a rough place and not just around the edges. Mark Twain's choice of book title, *Roughing It*, could not have been more apropos. *Wicked Virginia City* picks up where Twain left off by looking more closely at the seamier side of this vibrant and storied boomtown.

A Word on Bibliographic Citation

With a few exceptions, such as newspaper articles, full citations for sources quoted in this book are listed in the bibliography. The first time a source is mentioned within the text, the author, title and year of publication appear. Subsequent attributions are limited to the author's last name and year of publication.

ACKNOWLEDGEMENTS

Writing a book, as most authors will tell you, is a collective effort, and I have gotten inspiration and encouragement from both the quick and the dead. The former group includes Michael "Bert" Bedeau; ZoAnn Campana; Sandra Hedicke Clark; Greg Crouch; Rick and Karen Dustman; Josh Galarza; Kim Grey; Kim Harris; Ron and Susan James; Bob Kautz; Arline LaFerry; McAvoy Layne; Anne Leek; Mike Makley; Mike Morley; Gary Noy; Cindy Southerland; and Elizabeth Tully. The latter group includes Dan De Quille, Alf Doten and Mark Twain.

I am indebted to a number of libraries and archives and their knowledgeable staff for help in locating just the right documents and photographs. Individuals who stand out in this regard include Natacha Faillers, Catherine Magee, Liz Moore and Kim Roberts. I also would like to thank the staff of the library at Western Nevada College in Carson City.

The illustrations that appear in this book come from the following sources: Library of Congress; Nevada Historical Society; Nevada State Library and Archives; and Special Collections Department, University of Nevada–Reno Libraries. In addition, photographer Robin Johnson supplied several contemporary images of Virginia City, and some images are from the author's collection.

Lastly, I want to thank Comma Coffee in Carson City for its writing ambience and Laurie Krill, my talented and energetic editor at The History Press.

INTRODUCTION

It is the story of the birth of the silver-mining industry in this country, and it portrays as well the most vigorous growth of that industry. The simple narrative is, in truth, not less marvelous than an Arabian tale…which drew a swarm of men to a desert avoided even by beasts, and how from this clue a thread of gold was traced to its hidden source, and treasures rivaling the fancied store of the young Aladdin were unveiled. Its scenes present the toil of placer miners in an isolated cañon, the search of prospectors for gold and silver, the discovery of a world-famous lode, the extraordinary migration called tersely the "rush to Washoe," the life of a turbulent mining camp, and its ultimate crystallization into a thriving city.

—Eliot Lord

The discovery and development of the Comstock Lode was Nevada's defining moment. It was similar to the California experience a decade earlier. The gold rush catapulted California past territorial status to full statehood in two and a half short years. It is worth remembering that when John Marshall found that famous gold nugget at Sutter's Mill on January 20, 1848, California and Nevada belonged to Mexico, and the Mexican-American War had not yet concluded.

For most of the 1840s and 1850s, northern Nevada was a place to be traversed, often with considerable difficulty. Emigrants bound for the Pacific Coast faced numerous hardships, not the least of which included the parched Great Basin and the daunting Sierra Nevada Range. The pace of westward migration quickened throughout the 1840s, with two notable

The Bonanza Road at Lake Tahoe, near Glenbrook, circa 1860. *Courtesy of the Library of Congress.*

punctuations: the ill-fated Donner Party in 1846 and the discovery of gold in 1848. The Donner Party's experience instilled a sense of fear and respect for the mountainous barrier of the Sierra, the last hurdle at the western end of various emigrant trails. The gold discovery instilled just the opposite reaction—optimism and excitement, almost to the point of reckless abandon, for the so-called argonauts seemed blind to anything but the color gold.

By 1850, when California became a state and Utah became a territory, the valleys immediately east of the Sierra Nevada attracted the attentions of settlers. These included entrepreneurs who saw opportunity in provisioning emigrants, prospectors in search of mineral wealth comparable to California's Mother Lode and Mormon agriculturalists who wanted to settle the Carson Valley Mission. The 1859 discovery of the Comstock Lode in Nevada's Virginia Range stimulated unprecedented population growth.

The political consequences of the "Rush to Washoe," as this migration was called, included territorial status in 1861 and full statehood in 1864.

The mining rushes to California and Nevada fixed national attention on the western horizon. To be sure, Americans had been moving gradually west since the conclusion of the American Revolution, but the mass migration to West Coast mines was somehow different. The fertile valleys from the Appalachians to the eastern edge of the Great Plains were settled in an orderly fashion, and their umbilical-like connections were ultimately linked to East Coast centers of political and economic power.

The mining centers of the West Coast collectively constituted a political exclave; the region was, for all intents and purposes, a Pacific Rim nation with its own primate city: San Francisco. Some, like Henry David Thoreau, worried about the get-rich-quick motivation of miners and other opportunists and the type of society taking root on auriferous gravels and in underground ore bodies. Mining, according to their view, was deemed a lowly livelihood vis-à-vis more ennobling occupations, such as farming. The same sentiment is expressed in the title of one of the best histories of early Nevada, Sally Zanjani's *Devils Will Reign: How Nevada Began* (2006).

DISCOVERY AND DEVELOPMENT OF THE COMSTOCK LODE

The discovery of the Comstock Lode did not elicit a sudden aha moment like John Marshall plucking a gold nugget out of a mill race on the American River, which began the California gold rush. Instead, prospectors working the gravels of a south-facing canyon of Sun Mountain (the earlier name for the Comstock's Mount Davidson) for most of the 1850s realized a slow and steady return of gold.

History records that members of Mormon wagon trains, including one Abner Blackburn, were the first people to find flecks of gold in the vicinity. They worked the gravels upstream in a ravine they called Gold Canyon but were generally disappointed. Blackburn wrote in his diary in the spring of 1849, "We scrached [*sic*], scraped, and paned until nearly sundown and took out nine or ten dollars' worth of gold." That could hardly compare with what placer miners were finding on the California side of the Sierra.

In part, the environment was to blame for the hardship of mining in Nevada as compared to mining in California. The most important ingredient of placer mining was water, whether sand and gravels were washed with a simple pan or with more complicated contraptions. Because of the rain shadow effect, precipitation is much greater on the west side of the Sierra Nevada Range than on the east side, which accounts for Nevada's desert-like conditions. In addition, northern Nevada's elevations are higher, which makes winters there much more severe than they are in California's foothills at the same latitude. For example, Coloma, California, the site of Marshall's gold discovery, has an elevation of 764 feet above sea level, as compared to Virginia City's elevation of 6,148 feet.

Eliot Lord's authoritative book *Comstock Mining and Miners* (1883), which was initially published by the U.S. Geological Survey, shows that Gold Canyon placer miners numbered more than one hundred during the 1850s. It was a precarious and not-too-profitable existence, however, with their earnings averaging around four to five dollars per day. Among those men who persisted in Gold Canyon rather than heed the siren's call of California's Mother Lode, where miners were averaging twenty dollars per day, there were several whose names stand out as originators of the lode: the Grosh brothers, James "Old Virginny" Finney and Henry T. "Pancake" Comstock. What made the ill-fated brothers, Ethan Allen and Hosea Grosh, stand out was their recognition that another precious metal aside from gold existed on Sun Mountain. They found a silver deposit in a quartz vein matrix in 1856, which, in a sense, foreshadowed the Big Bonanza of silver discovered some years after their untimely deaths.

The Grosh brothers were not your typical gold-rush prospectors, insofar as they had a working knowledge of metallurgy, which was useful in recognizing silver. Unlike gold, silver will combine with other minerals. A gold nugget maintains its metallic color and is easily spotted in stream beds, sometimes called auriferous gravels. Silver, on the other hand, can take on many disguises as it binds with other minerals. (Early miners used to call this silver in its natural state "the annoying blue stuff.") In their book *The Gold Rush Letters of E. Allen Grosh and Hosea B. Grosh* (2012), authors Ronald James and Robert Stewart wrote, "The brothers were…something of an anomaly when they arrived in the profitable Great Basin placer district to prospect for rock-bound veins of precious metal." Unfortunately, the brothers did not live to see their discovery materialize into the underground mines of the Comstock Lode, as they both died tragically in 1857. In August of that year, Hosea accidentally struck himself in the foot with a pick and died of blood poisoning. Ethan Allen died as the result of frostbite he got while trapped in a Sierra snowstorm in November.

James Finney had the sobriquet of "Old Virginny" because he was a native of the state of Virginia. Virginia City is named for him and deservedly so, for "Old Virginny" is recognized as one of the discoverers of the Comstock Lode in January 1859, along with Alec Henderson, John Bishop and Jack Yount. Legend has it that Finney tripped while drunk, broke a bottle of whiskey he was carrying and thus baptized the city that bears the name of his home state. According to Zanjani (2006), "It seems fitting that this tough reprobate of a prospector, undeterred by hardship and complete isolation, living on whiskey and hope, is now recognized as Nevada's first permanent settler." In 1861, "Old Virginny" was thrown from his horse, some say while roaring drunk, and died. He was buried in the Dayton Cemetery.

Henry T. "Pancake" Comstock was another prospector whose name became immortalized, although he himself never realized any wealth. In June 1859, Patrick McLaughlin and Peter O'Riley were prospecting way up Six Mile Canyon, which, like Gold Canyon, has its origin on the upper slopes of Sun Mountain. After constructing a small earthen dam along a drainage, they began placer mining some unusual black rocks and discovered gold. That was precisely when "Pancake" Comstock rode up on his horse and demanded that he be included in the claim. Even more outrageous, Comstock insisted his friend Immanuel "Manny" Penrod, who was not present at the time, be included. Amazingly, McLaughlin and O'Riley acquiesced. Comstock's moniker, "Pancake," came from his explanation that he was too busy to bake bread, but some said he was just too lazy. The latter is more believable, given his willingness to horn in on the efforts of McLaughlin and O'Riley.

These discoveries in Gold Canyon and Six Mile Canyon prompted many miners to relocate from their settlements along the Carson River, catalyzing the births of the twin communities of Gold Hill and Virginia City. Gold Hill was initially the larger of the two, and it was where, on June 11, 1859, a group of miners assembled to create a mining district with its own laws governing mining claims. The assembly also elected officials: a justice of the peace, a constable and, most importantly, a recorder. The recorder's book became a sacrosanct record of who owned what claims within the mining district.

California Gold Rush to Comstock Mining

Almost immediately after the strikes of 1859, the Comstock changed from a loosely organized collection of prospectors and placer miners to a corporate structure in which miners worked for wages underground. The period of sifting through auriferous gravels and finding "pay dirt" ended, and it was replaced by exploring and extracting underground seams and ore bodies containing gold and silver. Because of the great expense involved—sinking shafts and tunnels deep underground, lining them with timbers, removing ore and waste rock, draining groundwater, pumping fresh air to miners, transporting and milling ore and casting bullion—mining companies backed by investors dominated the scene.

To fully appreciate mining on the Comstock Lode—the lifeblood of the boomtown of Virginia City—some understanding of the California gold rush antecedents is beneficial. Placer mining was the first type of mining practiced during the California gold rush. The Spanish word *placer*, meaning a type of non-vein free gold, became the standard term for both the geologic deposit and the technology used to obtain it (as well as the name of a California county in the Mother Lode).

James Marshall's discovery of loose gold in the American River prompted others to search similar active stream channels and their floodplains. It was soon discovered that gold tended to accumulate in areas where stream velocities changed abruptly from high to low energy. Because gold is a dense and heavy metal, it quickly drops out of a stream's suspended or bed sediment load with lowering energy. Nuggets and other particles were commonly found lodged in protective crevasses on the downstream side of boulders and mixed in with the fine sands that build up on the inside curve of a meander.

At first, many prospectors simply dug out the gold with large hunting knives. This worked well for the visible gold nuggets, but miners soon found that panning the fine sands, especially the black sands, could yield respectable returns on their labor in the form of particulate gold "dust." The basic design of the gold pan, a wide and shallow receptacle, allowed placer miners to scoop up a quantity of sand and water and deftly swirl it until only gold remained in the pan. Centrifugal force and the relative weight of gold did the trick. Finding gold remaining in the pan was known as "getting the color."

Gold panning itself was replaced in short order with "rockers" and somewhat later with "long toms" and "sluices." They all operated

Gould and Curry miners, 1870. *Courtesy of the Special Collections Department, University of Nevada–Reno Libraries.*

in accordance with the concept that gold could easily be trapped by a series of horizontal strips, or riffles, within a sloping box-like frame. The efficiency of gold retention increased by the addition of a pool of mercury on the upslope side of each slat. This was possible because mercury, or "quicksilver," can dissolve and keep in suspension small flecks of gold that would otherwise be swept away. The gold in the solution was easily recovered by heating the mercury, which then vaporized, leaving the gold. This process has been done since medieval times and underscores the importance of mercury in the recovery of precious metals.

Water was a vital ingredient in the placer mining process, and this posed a problem for Western miners. California has a Mediterranean-type climate (wet winters and dry summers), and Nevada is largely an arid desert. This meant that miners frequently had to contend with the scarcity or complete lack of water for their pans, rockers, long toms and sluices.

Hardrock mining, sometimes called quartz mining, began in 1849, when a quartz vein containing gold was discovered at Mariposa at the southern end of the Mother Lode. The difficulties involved in hardrock mining, when compared to the relative ease of processing auriferous gravels, dissuaded most miners from engaging in this form of mining for several years. Hardrock mining gained credibility in the latter half of the 1850s, when its associated technology improved. It also looked more attractive to

J. Ross Browne illustration, "Stand Aside, Gents!" *Author's collection.*

many miners who were aware that the Mother Lode's more easily worked placers would soon be exhausted.

There were three fundamental steps to hardrock mining: extracting the ore and waste rock, crushing the ore and recovering the precious metal. The first step was actually the simplest. Quartz veins were followed by digging down into solid rock, along the vein or "lode." Judiciously placed charges of gunpowder (later dynamite) facilitated excavation. Actually, the digging process entailed the sequential tasks of drilling holes to accommodate the powder, setting off the blast, "mucking" out the resultant chunks of ore and rock matrix (waste rock) and shoring up the shaft (vertical excavation) or adit (horizontal excavation) with timbers where needed. This process repeated itself as was necessary or practical.

Once both the ore and waste rock were removed from the mine, the waste rock was cast aside and the ore was sent to the crusher or mill. During the California gold rush, several devices accomplished this task. Two of these devices, the arrastra and the Chilean mill, were Latin American contributions with old-world antecedents. Both consisted of permutations on the theme of large rocks rotating on a rock floor or platform, crushing the ore between the two surfaces. A horse or mule attached to a pivoting harness and following a circular track generally provided the power. Early Comstock miners employed arrastras, but they proved inefficient and were incapable of processing large quantities of ore.

The mill of choice was the stamp mill. This device was composed of multiple upright pistons that raised and lowered onto a load of ore with a pulverizing effect. Gold recovery from crushed ore was more of a chemical process than a mechanical one. Importantly, it was the most vital of the three fundamental mining tasks—extracting, crushing and recovering—insofar as getting the gold through the first two processes did not necessarily guarantee recovery. Much depended on considerable chemical sophistication.

The contribution of the Comstock to the science and technology of mining was largely in the field of engineering. Deep underground hardrock mining there proved much more challenging than anything faced by California hardrock miners. The mines were deeper, hotter and more dangerous, and the solutions to these problems were true innovations. Many engineering works, such as Philipp Deidesheimer's square-set timbering system or Adolph Sutro's tunnel, facilitated underground mining. In addition, milling the Comstock gold and silver ore was improved by a homegrown method that became known as the Washoe Pan Process. Other engineering works in support of the Comstock included a long, inverted syphon that piped water in from the Lake Tahoe Basin and the Virginia and Truckee Railroad, which replaced the slow and costly wagon trains and connected the Comstock to the nation by rail.

Returning to the actual task of underground mining, one problem miners encountered was how to excavate large cavities of ore without risking a cave-in. These expansive excavations were known as "stopes," and a German-trained engineer Phillip Deidesheimer, who was working on the Comstock in 1860, solved the problem with the development of a timbering system that consisted of interlocking blocks. The blocks could be expanded to fill any void, and they were strong enough to support the roof and side walls of these manmade caverns.

Underground square-set timbering of Comstock Lode mines, 1876. *Illustration by T.L. Dawes. Courtesy of the Library of Congress.*

Adolf Sutro's tunnel was a good idea in theory, but by the time it was actually constructed, it was too little too late. As mines on the Comstock went deeper, several problems presented themselves. It became more difficult to get ore and waste rock out of a vertical shaft, getting fresh air for the miners to breathe became a greater challenge and many mines had to deal with pumping out water that seeped into the workings from underground aquifers. Sutro came up with a brilliant idea that would fix everything: the excavation of a tunnel coming in from the Carson River Valley, near Dayton, and intersecting the mine shafts at around 1,640 feet underground. Unfortunately, because of delays, it took almost nine years (1869–1878) to dig the nearly four-mile-long tunnel. By this time, many of the mines were deeper than the tunnel intersection. So, while the tunnel did provide additional ventilation and drainage, it did not live up to expectations of moving men and material.

Developments in milling technology took place all over the mining West, but the Comstock was clearly the industry leader. Innovations tended to originate or at least be refined in the many mills in the area. One important innovation became known as the Washoe Pan Process of amalgamation. The more complex ores, like the ones that existed on the Comstock, did not respond favorably to simple exposure to mercury, particularly because of their high contents of silver sulfide. Millers discovered that heating the ore with steam in large pans significantly increased the recovery of precious metals.

Another technological marvel associated with the Comstock was an inverted syphon that solved the problem of providing sufficient water to consumers and mills alike. There was water in the underground mines—in fact, too much water—but it was not fit for human consumption because of its mineral content, and mills could not use it without having to deal with mineral scale building up in their water systems. In 1871, the Virginia City Water Company hired Hermann Schussler, a German-born engineer who had recently designed a water conveyance system in the San Francisco area. Schussler designed and carried out an ambitious plan that involved piping water down from the Lake Tahoe Basin into the south end of Washoe Valley and back up into Virginia City. The force of gravity acted as a natural syphon, and the system delivered an abundance of fresh mountain water to the Comstock beginning in the summer of 1873. It was truly an astounding feat of engineering.

Finally, the Virginia and Truckee Railroad—also known as the Queen of the Short Lines or simply the V&T—was constructed by the directors of the Bank of California as a means of integrating their mining and milling investments with a transportation network. William Sharon, William C. Ralston and Darius O. Mills incorporated the Virginia & Truckee Railroad Company on March 5, 1868. Construction began in 1869, and three years later, the line connected with the transcontinental railroad in Reno by way of Carson City, thus providing a vital link to the larger world. The V&T was a challenge to construct; more than one thousand Chinese workers built its winding bed by slabbing hillsides and spanning steep ravines with trestles. The V&T outlasted the Comstock's mining boom by many years, finally making its last trip between Carson City and Reno on May 31, 1950.

BUILDING VIRGINIA CITY

In a few short years, Virginia City became a true city, with distinct neighborhoods and districts. Many of the residential neighborhoods were

Chollar, Norcross and Savage Shaft. *Photograph by R.J. Waters. Courtesy of the Nevada State Library and Archives.*

segregated along ethnic and class lines, and the districts—commercial, industrial and red-light—carved out their own spaces within the urban landscape. Gone for good were the scattered tents and dugout dwellings of egalitarian prospectors.

The new city adapted to the east-facing slope on which a grid of streets was superimposed. The principal streets, running roughly north to south, had alphabetic designations, with A Street lying at the greatest elevation and the subsequent letters given to the parallel streets downslope. The lettered streets corresponded with the slope contour so that they were relatively level. Cross streets, however, ran perpendicularly, so they were generally steep, much to the delight of boys sledding in the winter.

Mark Twain, a resident of Virginia City in the early 1860s, offered this visual in his book *Roughing It* (1872). "The fronts of the houses were level with the streets they faced, but their rear first floors were propped on lofty stilts; a man could stand at the rear first floor window on a C Street house and look down the chimney of the row of houses below him facing D Street." In his memoir, *An Editor on the Comstock Lode* (1936), Wells Drury further orients

International Hotel, circa 1890. *Photograph by James H. Crockwell. Courtesy of the Library of Congress.*

us by identifying the city center. "The central point of Virginia is at the intersection of C and Union streets. That is where C street is divided, the International Hotel being No. 1 North C street, and the Sawdust Corner saloon being No. 1 South C street. All the other streets running north and south are divided and numbered in the same way."

As it is today, C Street was the main thoroughfare and commercial district of Virginia City. In the city's early days, it also served as a dividing line between the upper and lower parts of town in an economic sense. Above C Street was where the more affluent residents lived. In fact, part of the upslope side of South B Street was called "Millionaires Row" because of its elegant houses, the most notable of which was the home of mine superintendent Robert Graves. This massive Second Empire–style house was built in 1868 and is still called "The Castle." Other notable houses in the affluent upslope part of Virginia City include the A Street home of opera house owner John Piper. Below C Street was where the other half lived. Virginia City's main red-light district was located on D Street, immediately north of Union, which was convenient to the many saloons one street above. Mary McNair Matthews, a widow who lived in Virginia City during the Big Bonanza and who later published her memoir, *Ten Years in Nevada or Life on the Pacific Coast* (1880), had this to say, "D Street was the condemned part of the city, being a street that no decent person lived on, at least but few north of Taylor Street. The south end is all occupied by respectable people."

"The Castle," home of mine superintendent Robert Graves, built in 1868. *Courtesy of Robin Johnson.*

"Chinese Quarters, Virginia City, Nevada." *Drawing by W.A. Rogers,* Harper's Weekly, *December 29, 1877. Courtesy of the Special Collections Department, University of Nevada–Reno Libraries.*

Virginia City also had a sizeable Chinatown further downslope. Described as a "narrow-laned shantytown," or worse in accordance with predominating prejudice, Chinatown was an ethnic enclave located between G and K Streets and bisected by Union Street. Chinatown existed on the margin of society and the settled landscape. Only a small Paiute settlement farther down Six Mile Canyon was more peripheral.

The industrial district dominated the landscape in a crescent shape, from the Ophir Pit in the north, east down Mill Street and south to the Combination Shaft. The shaft headframes, mill buildings with smokestacks, piles of waste rock and stacks of cordwood and mining timbers were visible from any vantage point. The sounds of this industry, in the words of Ronald James, the author of *The Roar and the Silence: A History of Virginia City and the Comstock Lode* (1998), "produced a twenty-four-hour cacophony that serenaded the Comstock."

Within this context, Virginia City, during the boom years, possessed numerous institutional outlets for the fulfillment and expression of social, religious, recreational and educational needs. Although, initially, the town's saloons, gambling halls and other commercial establishments constituted the only available options for social congregation, institutions, clubs and organizations began to proliferate and grow. Numerous voluntary social organizations also flourished in Virginia City. Fraternal organizations, such as the Knights of Pythias, the International Order of Odd Fellows and the Masons were especially popular. Virginia City had several fire companies, which, in addition to their obvious mission, doubled as civic organizations. Like the fire departments of today, these companies provided a considerable amount of camaraderie for their members and were indispensable in parades. Special interest organizations and venues also took root on the Comstock. For instance, Virginia City had a Miner's Union Hall on B Street. This organization, the Miner's Protective Association of Storey County, founded on May 30, 1863, was the first of its kind in the West. The union hall provided a two-thousand-volume library for the enjoyment of its members and their families.

Virginia City was not without its religious institutions and schools. Several churches, chief among them St. Mary's (Catholic), St. Paul's (Episcopal) and First Presbyterian, offered regular services to the religious. With the arrival of families in the early boom years, providing for the children's education became a concern. By 1865, Virginia City had seven public schools. One of Virginia City's landmarks is the impressive Second Empire–style Fourth Ward School, which operated from 1876 to 1936.

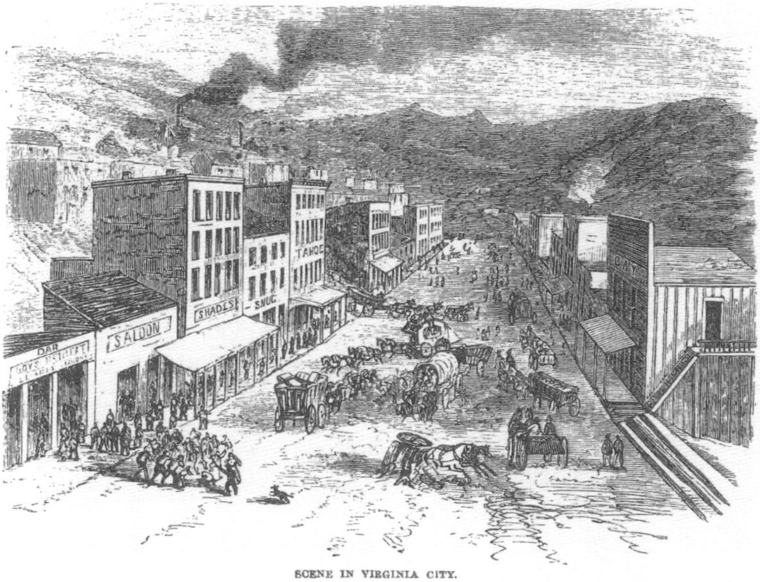

J. Ross Browne illustration, "Scene in Virginia City." *Author's collection.*

Piper's Opera House, 1950. *Courtesy of the Special Collections Department, University of Nevada–Reno Libraries.*

Opera houses were popular in many mining towns in the West, and Virginia City was no exception. Virginia City's best-known and preserved opera house is John Piper's Opera House on B Street. Piper's Opera House was the venue for a variety of crowd-pleasing attractions, such as dramatic performances, lectures, concerts, boxing matches and even fights between large wild animals. Well-known performers, such as Buffalo Bill, Lillie Langtry and John Philip Sousa and his band, also appeared here.

1
ALL THE NEWS THAT'S (UN)FIT TO PRINT

Ivory towers were few and far between in the American West. Beautiful letters almost invariably had to be translated into pork chops and rent; and this, together with the universally admitted affinity of printer's ink for whisky, strongly conditioned the literature of the time. Without any exception worth the naming, all Nevada literature of the nineteenth century was the literature of journalism. Every writer one can name in the time and place wrote for a newspaper or other periodical, even though he might eventually achieve the dignity of boards.
—*Lucius Beebe*

From our vantage point in the twenty-first century, it is hard to imagine life without electronic and satellite communication. During Virginia City's nineteenth-century heyday, however, almost everyone relied on print media—newspapers and magazines—for current events and entertainment. This was the golden age of print communication, and newspapers were king. Major metropolitan newspapers, such as Horace Greeley's *New York Tribune*, were regarded with reverence, and their publishers, editors and writers were minor celebrities.

Residents of the Comstock Lode loved their newspapers. Foremost among them were the *Territorial Enterprise*, which was printed in Virginia City from 1860 to 1893 and was regarded as the paper of record, as was its rival the *Gold Hill News*. Papers with lesser circulations and lifespans included the *Daily Democratic Standard*, the *Old Paiute*, the *Daily Safeguard*, the *Nevada Pioneer*, the *Occidental*, the *Trespass*, the *Virginia Daily Union*, the *Virginia Evening Bulletin*,

Local reporters, including Dan De Quille (*center*) and Alf Doten (*right*), 1865. *Courtesy of the Special Collections Department, University of Nevada–Reno Libraries.*

the *Virginia Evening Chronicle* and the *Washoe Daily Evening Herald*. There were even some foreign-language papers, such as the German *Nevada Staats Zeitung* and the *Deutsche Union*.

Great or small, these Comstock newspapers printed what readers found most interesting. There was, of course, the practical information, such as stock quotes and mining developments, as well as advertisements, which were important sources of revenue for any paper. What actually aroused attention, however, were the sensational happenings that were duly reported in great and gory detail. According to Lucius Beebe, the author of *Comstock Commotion: The Story of the Territorial Enterprise* (1954), these newsworthy human-interest stories included "shootings and stabbings, infidelities, suicides, assaults, embezzlements, and excursions into lawlessness."

The following is an example of what sold newspapers on the boarded sidewalks of Virginia City. As luck would have it—if luck is the appropriate word—a reporter for the *Territorial Enterprise* witnessed a shocking suicide at the Sawdust Saloon. This description appeared in the January 29, 1879 edition of the newspaper.

> *Charles H. Fosgard, an engineer of the C&C shaft, committed suicide at 9:30 last evening, shooting himself through the head with a Colt's Navy revolver while seated in a game of farobank in the Sawdust Saloon. Mr. Fosgard seems to have been suffering for a long time from that fearful depression which sometimes seizes people in this section. It is particularly severe in persons of certain temperament and is very apt to increase with time.*

The newspapermen of the Comstock, like the cable news networks of today, recognized the correlation between a sensational story and public interest. The more horrific or bizarre the story, the better. Reporters combed the Comstock's saloons, jails, morgues and brothels for good copy. Joe Goodman, Dennis McCarthy, Charlie "Judge" Goodwin, Rollin Daggett, Sam Davis, James "Lying Jim" Townsend, William Wright (also known as Dan De Quille), Samuel Clemens (also known as Mark Twain), Alfred (Alf) Doten, Wells Drury, Clement Rice and Tom Fitch became household names because of their abilities to give the reading public what they wanted.

Sometimes, on a slow news day, readers were treated to a complete fabrication and a hoax. Most locals had come to expect such stories from the likes of Dan De Quille and Mark Twain. According to Thompson and West's *History of Nevada* (1881), which was edited by Myron Angel, "items of news were not always to be culled from events that transpired, and this deficiency was usually, or often at least, supplied from the fertile brain of the reporter." For example, De Quille's story "The Traveling Stones of Pahranagat Valley," which was about rocks in the desert rearranging themselves in response to some unexplained physical force, was reprinted way beyond the borders of Nevada. The story prompted a group of learned scientists in Germany to write with enthusiasm for more information.

Samuel Langhorne Clemens, also known as Mark Twain. *Courtesy of the Library of Congress.*

Mark Twain perpetrated his share of hoaxes while he was a staff writer for the *Territorial Enterprise*. It seems Twain and De Quille tried to outdo one another in both hilarity and stretched credulity. One of Twain's best stories—"The Petrified Man"—was published in the October 4, 1862 edition of the *Territorial Enterprise*. It reads, "Every limb and feature of the stony mummy was perfect....The body was in a sitting posture and leaning against a huge mass of croppings; the attitude was pensive, the right thumb resting against the side of the nose." He followed up on the petrified man story a month later, adding, "A skillful assayer has analyzed a small portion of dirt found under the nail of the great toe and pronounces the man to have been a native of the Kingdom of New Jersey."

Competition among newspapers delighted Virginia City's reading public, insofar as feuds in print occasionally erupted into actual physical altercations. It was not uncommon to hear one offended party or another demand the satisfaction of a duel with pistols on a field of honor. *Territorial Enterprise* publisher Joe Goodman famously shot Tom Fitch of the *Virginia Daily Union* in the knee with a .44-caliber Colt revolver. Fitch walked with a limp for the remainder of his days. Another *Enterprise* man, Steve Gillis, is said to have survived three duels.

Even Mark Twain came within a hair's breadth of shooting it out with James Laird, the editor of the *Virginia Daily Union*. It was a hoax and a duel, in fact, that forced Mark Twain to flee both the *Enterprise* and Virginia City. In May 1864, Twain poked fun at a group of ladies in nearby Carson City who held a charity ball to raise money for the Sanitary Commission, which later became the Red Cross. The ball realized the substantial sum of $3,000 that was destined to aid wounded Union soldiers. Twain wrote, "The money raised at the Sanitary Fancy Dress Ball, recently held in Carson for the St. Louis Fair, had been diverted from its legitimate course and was to be sent to aid a Miscegenation Society somewhere in the East." He later recanted, writing in part, "The rumor was a hoax....However, four ladies are offended. We cannot quarrel with ladies—the very thought of such a thing is repulsive; neither can we consent to offend them, even unwittingly—without being sorry for the misfortune and seeking their forgiveness, which is a kindness we hope they will not refuse."

Twain's apology was not accepted, at least by a Virginia City newspaperman who came to the defense of Carson City's women. James Laird's *Virginia Daily Union* printed a scathing rebuke of Twain, calling him, among other things, a "vulgar liar." Twain responded in kind in the *Enterprise*. The inevitable duel arranged, Twain and his seconds, Steve Gillis and Rollin Daggett, arrived first at the field of honor on the outskirts of Virginia City. Just as Laird and his seconds were riding up, Gillis handily plugged a bird right in front of them and quickly handed the smoking pistol to Twain, loudly praising the marksmanship of the would-be duelist. That was enough to send Laird off on a suddenly remembered errand.

Dueling in America had its heyday in the first half of the nineteenth century, especially in the Southern states, but the bloody Civil War seemed to turn public sentiment against the *Code Duello*. By 1864, lawmen on the Comstock began to go after suspected duelists, and soon after word got out about a shot fired by Mark Twain, a warrant was issued for his arrest. Territorial governor James Nye, a friend of both the Clemens family and the *Territorial Enterprise*, let it be known that the warrant would not be acted upon for twenty-four hours, and it was strongly suggested that the *Enterprise*'s cub reporter skedaddle. Twain took the next stage bound for San Francisco, which actually turned out to be a godsend for his writing career.

Most barbs exchanged between rival newspapermen, in fact, did not result in violent confrontation. A camaraderie of sorts usually existed, whereby the true emotion behind an insult in print was admiration. Mark Twain, for instance, always referred to Clement Rice as "The Unreliable," and described him as "a reptile endowed with no more intellect, no more cultivation, no more Christian principle than animates and adorns the sportive jackass rabbit of the Sierras." In reality, the two had a great deal of respect for one another.

As exciting as it was to have newspapermen fighting among themselves, it was much more common to have offended parties among the reading public go after editors and reporters. Admittedly, rival papers on the Comstock resorted to sensational journalism in order to sell papers, and that meant entertaining readers with sometimes humorous, even libelous, caricatures and ad hominem. Barbs and ridicule became an accepted part of Sagebrush Journalism, the term ascribed to this school of Nevada news reporting.

When Alf Doten, editor of the *Gold Hill News*, hired Wells Drury, his advice to the cub reporter came with a warning: "You write what you please. Nobody censors it. But you must defend *yourself*, if anybody has a kick." Shortly thereafter, young Drury had occasion to deal with a malcontent who was supposedly slandered by Doten. The man, whom Drury described as "a great, hulking fellow," was apparently none too pleased with a piece in the *News* and explained his intent to get either an apology or satisfaction. As the man advanced on the cub, Drury reached for a revolver in the desk drawer. Unfamiliar with its hair-trigger, a shot rang out, and the glass door to one side of the hulk exploded. The would-be assailant made a hasty retreat and never again darkened the door of that, and perhaps any other, newspaper office.

Another incident involved one Thomas Williams, a Virginia City attorney who had made a pile of money on Con-Virginia stock and wanted to run for a seat in the U.S. Senate. *Territorial Enterprise* editor Rollin Daggett had written an unflattering piece, which prompted Williams to burst into the newspaper's office on C Street with a loaded gun. Looking into the abyss of the gun barrel, the editor hastily explained that a lawyer named Peters had written the offensive article. Williams stormed off, and a little while later, a visibly shaken Peters came into the *Enterprise* building and confronted Daggett. The explanation he offered did little to mollify Peters, but doubtless, it was true. "[Williams] burst in sudden-like and most intemperate of speech. Threatened to shoot me, in fact. I had to pass the buck to someone and you were the first son of a bitch that came to mind."

There also existed some good-natured bantering between members of the Fourth Estate and the reading public. The tale of Joe Goodman's conversation with a man reading a rival paper in a Virginia City thirst parlor is almost certainly apocryphal but funny nonetheless. Goodman asked the man on the stool next to him at the Sazerac Bar why he was reading the *Old Paiute*. The fellow recognized Goodman as the publisher of the *Territorial Enterprise* and decided to have a little fun. "I read the *Piute* to get the news. I use the *Enterprise* to wipe my behind." Not one to take the bait and without missing a beat, Goodman replied, "Keep right on as you are, friend, and in a short time, your behind will know more than your head ever will."

A SAMPLING FROM THE *TERRITORIAL ENTERPRISE*

The *Territorial Enterprise* is Nevada's oldest newspaper, having debuted in Genoa in 1858 before moving to Virginia City in October 1860. It quickly became the paper of record, insofar as it had the greatest influence of any paper in the state during the Gilded Age. An op-ed piece could sway public opinion on issues large and small. It could also make or break political aspirations, as William Sharon clearly knew when bought the paper in 1874 in order to facilitate his bid for a U.S. Senate seat.

What follows is a sampling of pieces published in the "Local Matters," later called the "Local Intelligence," section of the *Enterprise*. These are culled from a nearly complete collection of the newspaper on microfilm at the Nevada State Library and Archives in Carson City. They represent a

Territorial Enterprise composing room. *Courtesy of the Special Collections Department, University of Nevada–Reno Libraries.*

wide range of topics, but their common denominator is as illustration of the boisterous boomtown that was Virginia City in the 1860s and 1870s.

> *Theives About—Night before last, a gentleman of "industrie" had the kindness to clean the clothes line of Mr. Duval of everything except "diapers." These the thief had not the heart to take. Mr. Duval wishes to say to the thief that another washing will be hung out upon the same line on Friday next, and that he will be welcome to come back and take whatever will please his fancy. (May 6, 1866)*

> *Dog Fight—A very eligible and interesting dog fight took place in front of Gillig, Mott & Co.'s on C street yesterday evening, which was well attended by admiring spectators. It seemed to be a free fight, from our stand-point of view, there being some four dogs pitching in together with a perfect looseness, while our little dog, Kyzer, sparred furiously round on the outside, biting savagely at any stray hind leg or tail that he came across. (May 10, 1866)*

> *"Rattlesnake Dick" Arrested—A somewhat noted individual calling himself by the above cognomen was arrested day before yesterday in this city for inveigling money and a watch out of a lady with whom he was*

a passenger on the stage from Austin a few days ago. Dick, on obtaining possession of the above, starts out on a grand spree, when the money soon vanished, and the watch was put in soak. The lady had been started by her husband on a visit to the States. The next morning, Dick was arrested and in default of $500 bail was snugly quartered in the county jail, where he remains. (May 16, 1866)

Belligerent—Yesterday morning, a couple of individuals got into a bit of a quarrel together in front of Kirk & Co.'s drugstore on C street, which resulted in one trying to cane the other and the other drawing a six-shooter. Constable Ash interfered, stopped the muss and arrested the parties. (May 22, 1866)

A Foul Piece Of Business—Yesterday noon, a man was terribly beaten and mangled about the head at a well-known drinking saloon on South C street, nearly opposite the Occidental, by parties unknown. We visited the scene shortly afterwards. (May 26, 1866)

Daring Highway Robbery—About 9 o'clock, night before last, Lieutenant Ed Ingham connected with the Kelsey Mill, Silver City, was on his way up to Gold Hill in a buggy, together with his wife and child, when shortly after having passed the Devil's Gate, he was stopped by four "road agents," well armed, one or two with shotguns, who commanded him to "stand and deliver." Ingham was unarmed, taken by surprise, and having his wife and child with him, he could not well do otherwise than "shell out," so he delivered up a purse of $190 in coin, and was in the act of also passing over his gold watch when they told him: "Go to hell with your watch, we don't want it." Mr. Ingham drove at once to Gold Hill and told the police and others, who started out in pursuit but without success thus far. (June 2, 1866)

No Business—No business in the criminal line came up yesterday in either of our justices' courts. All is quiet along the "Pottymack." (March 24, 1870)

Drunks—Several drunks were reeling around town last night, but they were not of the fighting order, and no arrests were made. (January 10, 1873)

Fined—One James Breen, having devoted nearly the whole day to worshipping at the shrine of Bacchus, succeeded in raising his spirits to an *explosive pressure, and the kindly attention of officer Simpson was rendered necessary to convey him to a place of safety. Judge Marple, yesterday, assessed him to the amount of $15. (January 15, 1873)*

WOMEN ON THE WAR-PATH—About 12 o'clock night before last, two women had a lively fight on B street in front of the Masonic block. Chignons suffered terribly. The way they clawed each other would have astonished the most experienced tomcat in the land. Sometimes one and sometimes both were down—the slippery sidewalk affording but very insecure footing—but they only fell to rise again more wrathful than before. Yesterday morning, it is said that that portion of the sidewalk, which was the scene of the battle, was all red with—hair. (February 22, 1873)

POLICE BUSINESS LIVELY—Night before last was very lively for the policemen. No less than twelve arrests were made, principally for disturbing the peace and for being drunk and disorderly. Most of the arrests were made on South C Street in the direction of the Divide—that section of the town known as the "Barbary Coast." (March 11, 1873)

HAPPY CELESTIALS—The Chinese wood-peddlers were, yesterday, the happiest men in town. With their donkeys loaded with wood, they were seen climbing the steep cross streets and scouting out in all directions in search of their customers. With them, stocks were up, and their bonanza was on the bulge. (January 15, 1875)

IMMIGRATION—Numbers of people from all parts of the United States, attracted by the reports which have gone out concerning the great ore deposits of the Comstock, are flocking to Virginia. Among the newcomers is a plentiful sprinkling of people from far-off Maine. The new arrivals belong, as a general thing, to an industrious, thrifty class and will no doubt, in due time, come in for their full share of the treasures wrested from the bowels of the earth. (February 23, 1875)

A CORONER'S INQUEST—An inquest has been held by Coroner Mayer in the matter of the human remains lately found in the old shaft on the claim of the East Comstock Mining Company. The inquest was held in order to see what light could be obtained in regard to the matter of finding human remains in such a place.... The verdict of the jury was that the remains were those of a man whose name was to them unknown, and the matter was left open in order to see if something might not be found in the shaft that would furnish a clue which could be followed up. (March 14, 1875)

IMPOSTER AND CONFIDENCE MAN—That is the way the dispatches set him up. He was first noticed by Officer Sheehan of Gold Hill about 5 o'clock on Sunday morning, while he was endeavoring to get a saddle horse of O.C. Mundell of that place with the intention of going to Wadsworth. Word was immediately brought to Chief of Police Lackey, who went to Gold Hill and identified the man as Alexander Craig, alias Morris Daley, known as "the confidence man," who escaped from the Solano County (California) Jail, April 19, 1875, and for whose apprehension a reward of $50 is offered by the sheriff of that county. (April 28, 1875)

NOT SO—Mrs. Bowers, often mentioned as the "Washoe Seeress," who is now in this city, denies that she ever predicted the destruction of the Grand Hotel, San Francisco, by an earthquake. She also denies having predicted that an earthquake would occur within six months in San Francisco. She is very much annoyed by the stories that have been put in circulation in regard to her having predicted an earthquake when she has never for a moment thought of such a thing. This being the case, those who have moved out of the Grand Hotel may move back without fear of being shaken out of their boots. (August 3, 1876)

MIKE MCGOWAN—The man-eater, and a few other prisoners who refuse to work out their own deliverance when sentenced to a term in the Virginia City Jail, are very properly kept upon a diet of bread and water. The prisoners who take up the pick and shovel have good food in plenty and are allowed two days off their term for every day they work. (September 5, 1876)

CUTTING AFFRAY—At 4:30 yesterday afternoon, a cutting affray occurred on the back porch of Piper's Row, between D and E streets, near Union, in which Nicolas Zamora received several severe cuts on the head from Phil Durand. The trouble commenced in the restaurant right below when the parties were ordered out. They then adjourned to the porch. When discovered, Durand was cutting away at Zamora's head with a jack-knife. Not satisfied with the effects produced in this way, he shut up the knife, put it in his pocket, seized an iron bar and continued operations. Zamora's head showed some five or six extended scalp wounds, which bled profusely but which are not dangerous. A warrant was issued for Durand's arrest. (July 10, 1877)

New Volume—With today's issue, the Enterprise enters upon its thirty-fifth volume. For eighteen years, it has daily given greeting to the men of Nevada. The efforts of its several managers to make it worthy the splendid people who are its readers have been most generously appreciated. It was here a prosperous institution when the state of Nevada was born; we trust it will remain, with increasing prosperity and usefulness, as long as the state exists. (August 1, 1877)

A Supposed Professional—An old woman has been engaged in begging in this city for some days—about the mines and in other places—who is supposed to be one of the regular army of professional mendicants. Last Wednesday, she went to the office of one of our firms of brokers and bought $15 in greenbacks; at the same place, she bought $20 in currency on Thursday, and yesterday, she bought at the same office $45 in currency, making a total of $80 in three days.... She dresses in mourning and claims to be a widow residing in this city and having six children to support. Our free-handed miners should be sure that they are giving to worthy persons before parting with their hard-earned dollars. Let them give only to those they know are of this place and in need, and we shall have fewer professional beggars in the town. (August 4, 1877)

2

WHISKEY MILLS, BEER HALLS AND OPIUM DENS

Numerous advertisements in contemporary newspapers portray the assortment of saloons, including those that offered customers billiards, Havana cigars, female entertainment, dancing, coffee, cockfights, dogfights, and a range of alcoholic beverages.... Well paid miners worked hard underground during eight-hour shifts. They tended to have disposable income, and because of the shorter-than-usual workday, they had free time, especially during mining bonanzas. Saloons served as places where they could while away free time and spend money.

—Kelly J. Dixon

Comstock miners spent an inordinate amount of time in saloons, not simply for the drink, as some would surmise, but because these establishments were much more than thirst parlors. As Dixon observes in *Boomtown Saloons: Archaeology and History in Virginia City* (2005), the life of a miner was divided into thirds, and when they were not sleeping or working, the one hundred saloons in Virginia City beckoned. Many, if not most, saloons offered food, entertainment and a place to socialize and relax. Their welcoming atmosphere was not unlike that portrayed in the television sitcom *Cheers*, with the exception that everyone carried weapons, gambled and used colorful language.

One reason for the popularity of saloons in Virginia City was that many people lived in overcrowded boarding or lodging houses (the distinction being that the former served meals). These places maintained a rigid schedule, whereby residents, mostly unmarried miners, slept in shifts. Even the more

J. Ross Browne illustration, "Home for the Boys." *Author's collection.*

commodious houses that containing unshared rooms could be described as stark and small. Some boarding and lodging houses boasted parlors that provided a modicum of space for residents who were not sleeping or working, but for many of those residents, the society of C Street became a part of their daily routines.

The saloon, as a place to while away the hours between work and sleep, quickly became a tradition in Virginia City. In his memoir, Drury (1936), quoted his old friend and senior statesman of C Street, James "Kettle Belly" Brown, expressing an opinion on proper drinking behavior.

> *I was shocked to see three young men, one after the other, march into a drinking-place where I was enjoying a flagon of native burgundy and take their liquor raw.…The movement made by these young men as they tossed off the liquor was like that of the stage actor representing a Russian*

> *drinking vodka. Now, I have sampled that same vodka, and I must say that I don't blame a Russian or anybody else for getting rid of such a vile decoction as quickly as possible, but it is an insult to good American liquor to treat it that way.*

Kettle Belly's shock over the flagrant disregard for drinking protocol is illustrative of how saloons were viewed by the majority of patrons. Saloons were "homes away from home" for many men on the Comstock. They approximated, among other things, a lively living room full of camaraderie. Rushing in and tossing back a few alcoholic shots apparently disrupted conventional sensibilities.

Newspapers frequently published stories and advertisements promoting saloon amenities and ambience. The following February 9, 1867 *Territorial Enterprise* piece announcing the grand opening of the Express Billiard Saloon was fairly typical.

> *Charley Sturm and Mr. Muller, having gone into partnership, will hereafter run the above popular institution, in the basement of Wells, Fargo & Co.'s, together. The saloon has just been enlarged to twice its original size by cutting an arched passage through the brick partition which separated the two portions of the basement, and besides the other attractions of the place, in the way of choice lager and other good beverages, desirable lunch, etc., two fine billiard tables have been added. They will have a grand opening, or social reunion, this evening, with music and all sorts of fun. All their friends are invited to come, eat, drink and be merry.*

Although it is possible to generalize about the one hundred Virginia City saloons—they all provided a place to "eat, drink and be merry" for their mostly male patrons—there also existed an amazing diversity among these establishments. Some saloons and beer halls catered to a specific ethnic clientele, such as the Irish; some highbrow establishments drew their patrons from among the professional class, while at the opposite end of the economic spectrum, there were "one-bit saloons" that catered to a largely blue-collar clientele.

In *The Big Bonanza* (1876), Dan De Quille explains the "bit" as a form of currency common to Virginia City saloons. "The majority of these saloons are what are called 'bit houses'; that is, drinks of all kinds and cigars are one bit—twelve and one half cents. The dime, however, passes as a 'bit' in all of these houses." Mary McNair Matthews (1880), who never patronized a saloon, elaborated: "The Nevadans are no penny-mites. The smallest change is one dime, which they call a 'short bit'—12 cents being a 'bit,' 15 cents a 'long bit,' 25 cents 'two bits,' 50 cents 'four bits,' and 75 cents 'six bits.' A dollar is a dollar."

A major distinction existed between the one-bit and two-bit saloon. The term "two-bit" has a cheap connotation in the parlance of today, but in Virginia City, a two-bit saloon generally attracted a better class of clientele. Once again, De Quille (1876) explains:

> *The money in circulation is wholly gold and silver coin, and the smallest coin in use is the bit, or ten-cent piece—sometimes spoken of as a 'short bit,' as not being twelve and one half cents, the 'long bit.' There being no smaller change in use than the dime, the bit passes for the half of twenty-five cents. Thus, whenever a customer throws down a quarter of a dollar in payment for a drink or a cigar, he gets back a dime, and so has paid fifteen cents for his 'nip' or smoke....In the 'two-bit,' or twenty-five-cent saloons, everything is twenty-five cents, even the same drinks that are sold in the bit houses for ten cents, as lager beer, soda water, lemonade, cider, and the like.*

Regardless of social stratification among saloon clientele, as reflected in the price of a drink, Virginia City's thirst parlors did a brisk business. Trade was especially vigorous on the first of every month, when the mines disbursed thousands of dollars in pay.

ANTECEDENTS

Drinking establishments are known by many names in the English language—taverns, public houses, bars, beer gardens and saloons, among others. The word saloon comes from the French *salon*. Its original meaning was associated with a living room or a public hall; in America, it became a synonym for a bar, particularly with a western frontier connotation.

Doubtless, many Virginia City thirst parlors resembled the quintessential frontier saloon, with batwing doors, a blue haze of tobacco smoke, tinny piano music and men seated at the poker table or standing at the bar. Hollywood perpetuates this image—from early Westerns like *High Noon* (1952) to *Tombstone* (1993) and *The Kid* (2019)—to the extent that a saloon scene is a sine qua non of the Western genre. Regardless of this popular stereotype, Virginia City's saloons represented cultural institutions with roots in colonial America and the Old World.

Kelly Dixon (2005) briefly outlined the history of public drinking houses: "People have been enjoying public drinking places for a longer span of time and over a wider geographical range than the nineteenth-century American West." She traces their direct link to ancient Mesopotamia, Egypt, Greece and Rome and also explains how the English-style pub morphed into the tavern in colonial North America. The tavern may be thought of as the progenitor of the saloon. During the period leading up to the American Revolution, local taverns provided more than a rum toddy or a glass of Madeira; they were, in fact, public meeting places where a nation was conceived. With westward expansion, the town tavern, along with its important function as a gathering place, moved into newly settled areas. Somewhere along the way—between the Great Plains and the Pacific—saloons as we know them became an icon of the frontier.

Whiskey Mills and Beer Halls

Virginia City had the reputation of being a hard-drinking town. Thirst parlors, such as the Boston Saloon, Delta, Sawdust Corner, Sazerac, Union Brewery and Washoe Club, saw greater congregations than all the city's churches, clubs and opera houses combined. In 1880, Virginia City's per capita consumption of alcohol was estimated at 22.5 gallons per year—much of that whiskey—and that was considered a comparatively dry year. (Today, Nevadans annually consume 3.46 gallons of alcohol per capita per year.)

The city had its temperance societies, such as the Sons of Temperance and the Independent Order of Good Templars, which advocated the benefits of abstinence from alcohol. These organizations attained national popularity throughout the nineteenth century, but their membership and influence on the Comstock, where the saloon crowd held sway, remained minimal. According to James (1998), "Opposition to saloons and alcohol on the Comstock ultimately had little effect on the institution of drinking and the businesses that supported it."

Drinking was Virginia City's cherished pastime, and drinking to excess apparently did not carry much in the way of social stigma. On the contrary, someone in the state of utter inebriation could laugh through their hangover the next day and boast about what a good time they had the night before—whether they remembered it or not. Considered good for business, some saloonkeepers even offered their regular patrons a free drink in the morning; this was universally known as an "eye-opener" or "restorative." Saloonkeepers considered it "priming the pump." Needless to say, one Virginia City temperance initiative—"to prevent a [bartender] from selling over $5 worth of spirits to one man"—garnered limited support. Drury (1936) related the humorous story of a Gold Hill resident who had the reputation of being a devoted tippler. "Brutus…groaned when his wife accused him of being drunk twenty-seven nights in the preceding month, and who, when sharply interrogated by his spouse, explained that by his groans he was expressing sorrow for missing those other three nights."

Many of the early arrivals to Virginia City came from California's gold country, where saloons were among the first businesses established in mining camps. From Downieville in the north to Columbia in the south, embryonic saloons were nothing more than canvas tents vending whiskey by the glass. Virginia City's first saloon, which some say was its first business, was just such a rude establishment. Charlie Sturm's bar, situated on the southwest corner of A and Sutton Streets, consisted primarily of two boards propped up on barrels in the tradition of the California gold rush.

By the early 1860s, the city's thirst parlors had multiplied exponentially, keeping pace with the Rush to Washoe. They boasted the false-fronted architecture that was then popular and an interior décor not dissimilar to the C Street saloons of today. The standard bar contained an elegant mirrored-back bar, gaslights suspended from high tin ceilings, commodious brass spittoons, assorted tables and chairs and the ever-popular paintings of reclining semi-nude women.

Virginia City's saloons featured different forms of entertainment and ambience. O'Brien and Costello's Saloon on South C Street, for example, boasted a shooting gallery. As bizarre as that may sound, the combination of bar and shooting range enjoyed considerable patronage. William Brown's Boston Saloon on South D Street, which catered to an African American clientele, offered good home cooking and Dixieland jazz. Interestingly, an archaeological excavation of the site of the Boston Saloon unearthed the oldest-known Tabasco Pepper Sauce bottle. For patrons who sought a "tonier" place in which to imbibe, there was the bar at the International Hotel.

According to Drury (1936), "Some of the bars were well-conducted, others were riotous and disorderly houses." Among the riotous were those that featured hurdy-gurdy girls, who did floor shows or danced for a fee

J. Ross Browne illustration, "The Hurdy-Gurdy Girls." *Author's collection.*

with individual patrons, and their location, not surprisingly, was generally convenient to the brothels of D Street and the Barbary Coast. Saloons notorious for crooked gambling also became riotous on occasion—sometimes with fatal consequences.

Saloons served a variety of drinks in addition to whiskey, that icon of the Wild West. Beer was a popular beverage, and the Comstock was actually home to some twenty-six breweries, most of which were under the ownership or management of German brewers. The local breweries included the Bavaria, the California, the Hibernia, the Nevada, the Pacific, the Philadelphia, the St. Louis, the Union, the Virginia, the Washington and the Washoe. Writing in *Nevada in the West* magazine (2011), Eric Moody and Robert Nylen stated, "There is some evidence that the Virginia Brewery, a small wooden building, had been making beer since June [1860]." That would make the Virginia Brewery, which was established by John M. Flurshurtz and several other German immigrants, contemporaneous with Jacob Klein's Carson City Brewery, long considered the first brewery in Nevada.

Union Brewery, 1925. *Courtesy of the Special Collections Department, University of Nevada–Reno Libraries.*

Jacob Van Bokkelin. *Courtesy of the Nevada Historical Society.*

Virginia City's German-style beer gardens flourished in part because of their festive atmospheres. Beer could be—and was—consumed all over town, but places like Van Bokkelin's Beer Garden attracted a devoted clientele. Major General Jacob L. Van Bokkelin was one of Virginia City's leading citizens and a man of many talents. A Civil War veteran, he commanded the Virginia City National Guard and cut quite a figure in many parades down C Street. His beer garden made him a celebrity among Virginia City's German population, although he himself was an old knickerbocker of New York Dutch ancestry. Germans on the Comstock considered his establishment a community focal point that celebrated their ethnic heritage. It also appealed to a much wider clientele, and unlike some of the rougher saloons in town, it offered a family-friendly atmosphere. Contributing to the appeal of Van Bokkelin's Beer Garden was its suburban location down Six Mile Canyon.

In addition to running his beer garden, Van Bokkelin imported nitroglycerine and sold dynamite to Comstock mines. Unfortunately for Van Bokkelin and his neighbors, he stored the volatile explosive in his bedroom in a lodging house on B Street. On the evening of June 29, 1873, his inventory exploded with devastating results; the blast leveled the lodging house, and the general and at least nine of his neighbors perished. Following Van Bokkelin's untimely death, Louise Mackay, the wife of Bonanza King John Mackay, purchased the beer garden property and donated the land to the Daughters of Charity of Saint Vincent de Paul. The Catholic religious order subsequently built the St. Mary Louise Hospital on the land, and it served the community until 1897. The building now houses the St. Mary's Art Center. Interestingly, this venue has a Van Bokkelin Gallery, where art receptions include beer, wine and cheese. The good general was buried in the nearby Silver Terrace Cemeteries, and one would like to think that his spirit visits the gallery on occasion.

OPIUM DENS

Chinatowns throughout the West were ethnic enclaves where the immigrant Chinese community could feel somewhat insulated from the strange and sometimes hostile dominant society. They contained familiar foods, medical practitioners, religious shrines, barbers and merchants, as well as gambling dens, opium dens and houses of prostitution. In short, residents sought to replicate Chinese culture on foreign soil.

Mary McNair Matthews's memoir (1880) contains considerable vitriol where Virginia City's Chinatown is concerned. Although she makes innocuous statements, these are usually followed by expressions of disgust that employ the adjectives "loathsome," "filthy" and "pestilential." The widow Matthews (1880) was especially alarmed by the "pernicious habit" of opium smoking.

> *Their opium dens, which seem to defy all police power to break up, are a nuisance and are also ruining our people, for many have become slaves to this most destructive habit. But not only men and women visit the opium dens, but I am informed, by good authority, that girls and boys visit them and often have to be helped home by their companions. Girls and boys, from twelve to twenty, are daily being ruined by this opium smoking. I never*

Mary McNair Matthews.
Author's collection.

> *visited one of these dens, but have had them described to me. A table sets in the center of the room, a dish of opium upon that, and long pipes for each smoker is dipped in this, and they lie on bunks around the table and smoke 'till they become unconscious. After a person once smokes, he has created an appetite for a vice that he has no power or wish to refrain from. You who are so far from these scenes of vice have no idea of the baneful effects of this pernicious habit. It is utter ruin to smoke the first pipe, for there is but one way to keep them from it afterwards, and that is the walls of an asylum.*

Mary McNair Matthews's concern that the habit of opium smoking was gaining popularity among the wider non-Asian population of Virginia City had some validity. James (1998) wrote, "The Chinese community held the allure of the exotic and the dangerous, and many found its prostitutes and opium dens too seductive to resist." Speaking from personal experience, *Gold Hill News* editor Alf Doten made frequent mention in his journals about "whisky, opium, and general dissipation."

A double standard existed where opium was concerned. Non-Asians in Virginia City used opium in various forms with little or no social stigma. Many prescriptions and patent medicines of the day contained high levels of opium and its derivatives, laudanum and morphine. Doctors prescribed them and pharmacists dispensed them knowing full well their patients and customers, many of whom were "respectable" women and temperance supporters, had a substance abuse problem. In her chapter in *Comstock Women* (1998) titled ""The 'Secret Friend': Opium in Comstock Society, 1860–1887," Sharon Lowe cited the case of Annie Alchoon, "a Virginia City wife and mother, [whose] self-medication of laudanum and morphine became not only addicting, but fatal." Lowe pointed out that Mrs. Alchoon's case was not an isolated instance of self-medication, nor was she the only fatality. Smoking opium in Chinatown, on the other hand—even if recreationally and only occasionally—was frowned on by the gatekeepers of Virginia City's morality. Part of this social disapprobation derived from the simple act of associating with the Chinese, a group that was held in low esteem in the West of the late nineteenth century. A nocturnal sojourn to Chinatown, therefore, carried with it a sense of slumming and debauchery.

One frequent visitor who made the rounds in Chinatown was editor Alf Doten; he readily confided to his diary the activities he would be reluctant to commit to newsprint. One such entry from October 4, 1865, reads, in part, "Drank at Tom Poo's…went to Mary's house…laid on the bed with her and smoked opium.…On my way home, I stopped in at the Great Republic

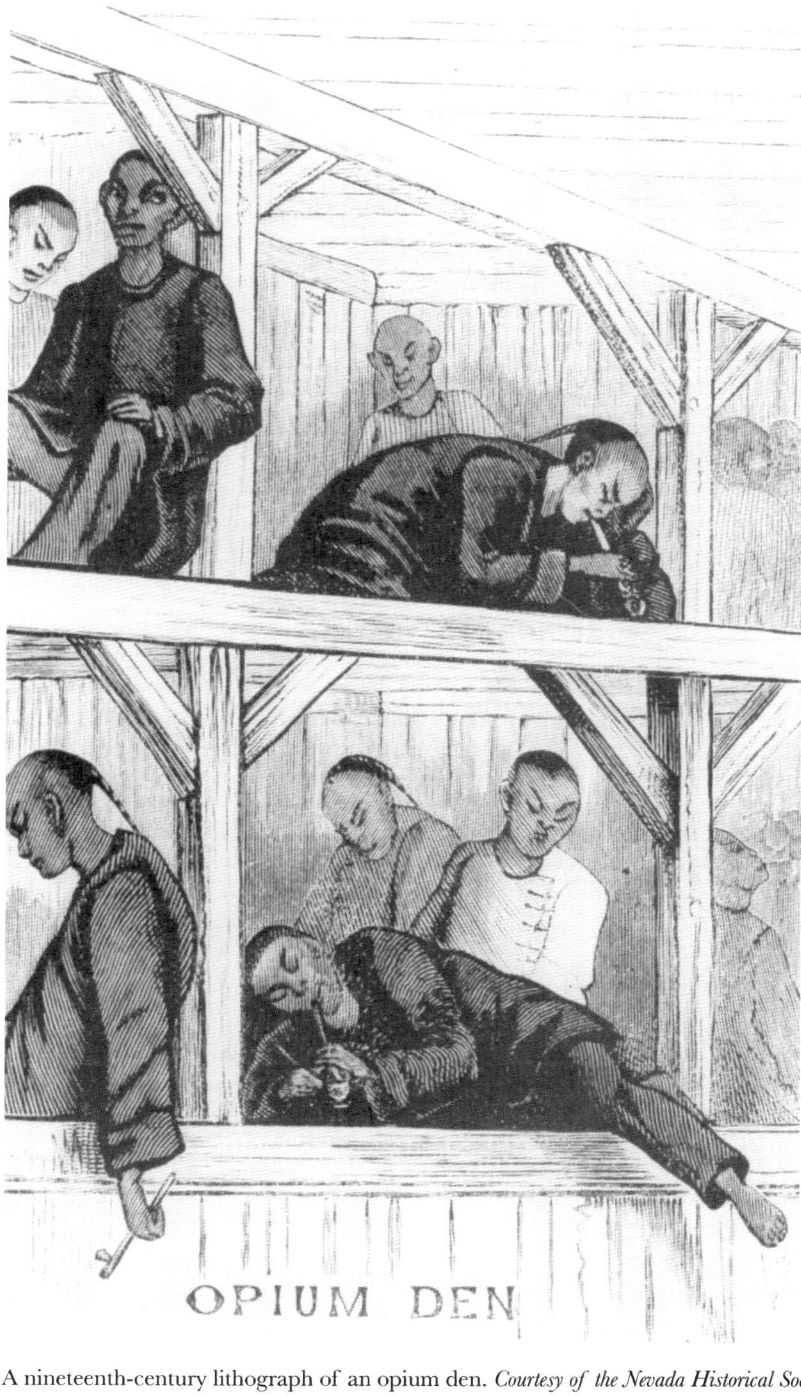

A nineteenth-century lithograph of an opium den. *Courtesy of the Nevada Historical Society.*

saloon—big whore ball going on." Doten apparently enjoyed, to use James's phrase, "the allure of the exotic."

The West was awash in opium during the early Comstock years. In 1870, Chinese companies in San Francisco legally imported some 2,413,073 pounds of the stuff, and opium dens in Virginia City never suffered a shortage of the narcotic. Writing in the *Nevada Historical Society Quarterly* (1981), Russell Magnaghi cited an illustrative example of supply and demand: "Sing Woh, an operator of a den at the corner of Union and H Streets observed that between 1871 and 1876, his annual purchases of opium had jumped from five and a half to over thirty-five pounds." At the height of the Big Bonanza, however, public sentiment in Virginia City rallied against the practice of opium smoking following a series of newspaper exposés. In its June 8, 1875 issue, for example, the *Virginia Evening Chronicle* opined, "There is no city on the coast where the Oriental custom of smoking opium is more thoroughly established than here or in which it is calculated to produce more destructive effects." Local and state ordinances outlawed opium dens in 1876 and specified penalties of up to $500 and six months in jail. The practice continued, albeit in more clandestine settings, like abandoned tunnels and cellars.

Drinking Buddies

Dan De Quille and Alf Doten

Two of the most celebrated Comstock pub crawlers were William Wright, who was universally known by his nom de plume, Dan De Quille, and Alf Doten. Thanks to the friendship of these two newspapermen, which was cemented by years of bending the elbow in the saloons of Virginia City and ferreting out a good story, we have a sense of the role saloons played in the lives of the residents of the Comstock Lode. The duo of De Quille and Doten spent their careers drinking and writing in more or less equal measure.

Much has been made of the friendship between Dan De Quille and Mark Twain, both of whom reported for the *Territorial Enterprise* and even roomed together for a time, but Twain's tenure on the Comstock only lasted two years. De Quille and Doten, however, became old-timers together. Except for short periods when De Quille visited his wife and children in Iowa, he was in Virginia City from 1860 to 1897. Doten arrived on the scene in 1863 and remained there until 1881, when he sold the *Gold Hill News* and moved

Left: William Wright, also known as Dan De Quille. *Courtesy of the Special Collections Department, University of Nevada–Reno Libraries.*

Right: Alf Doten. *Courtesy of the Special Collections Department, University of Nevada–Reno Libraries.*

to Austin, Nevada. In their respective oeuvres—especially De Quille's *The Big Bonanza* (1876) and Doten's *Journals*—we have an incomparable record of land and life on the Comstock during its heyday in intimate detail. All due respect to Mark Twain's *Roughing It* (1872), but critics agree that *The Big Bonanza* is the single best book about the Comstock Lode. Close seconds are the journals of Alf Doten; those seventy-nine bound journals cover the years between his arrival in California in 1849 and the day of his death in 1903. In 1973, after a decade of laborious transcription by Nevada writer Walter Van Tilburg Clark, the University of Nevada Press published this treasure trove that contains five decades of Western history.

Tragically, both De Quille and Doten's addiction to alcohol eventually ruined their health. In the case of Doten, alcoholism took a toll on his marriage and his newspaper career. The buddies were fully cognizant that their years of debauchery came with a price. De Quille had periods of sobriety, but temptation eventually prevailed. In 1897, Doten made this entry in his journal about De Quille: "used up generally that he cannot live long…can only walk about the house a little, grasping cane with both hands—has not been able to walk down from his residence on A street, Va, to C Street and back for nearly or quite 2 years—Looks to be 90 years old, yet was 68 on the 9th of May last."

While it lasted, the pair had a rollicking good time. The following is a selection from Doten on their drinking life in Virginia City.

> *Christmas Eve—Got all the Enterprise boys out—some 15 or 20 of us in all—Dan De Quille also along—visited all the saloons—free drink with all of them—printers on the rampage—even went down to Chinatown and kicked up thunder—came back—at 4 o'clock, Dan and I made out to get clear from the crowd and home to our beds. (December 24, 1863)*

> *At 4 o'clock, took passage with Dan De Quille on the California stage bound for Excelsior—whiskey gave out before reaching Donner Lake. (August 8, 1865)*

> *Considerable cruising with Dan…and others, including Bow Windows* [a Virginia City brothel], *a whore's ball at Millington's…and Chinatown. (January 3 through February 1, 1866)*

> *At Opera House—After that, I met…Dan De Quille, and we ran together, telling stories and drinking 'till daylight began to peep. (May 25, 1872)*

> *Dan De Quille has taken to drinking again the last three or four days after abstaining entirely for the past two years. (March 1, 1875)*

> *PM took a ride in buggy with wife out to the County Hospital—Met Dan De Quille—he has been there about 2 months from drinking and using himself bad, but is nearly ready to leave. (February 18, 1877)*

As newspapermen who drank heavily, Dan De Quille and Alf Doten were not alone. Among the Comstock's Fourth Estate, saloons were considered great places to get a story, and a trip to the nearest thirst parlor after the paper was put to bed was a nightly ritual. De Quille and Doten may have embraced that aspect of their job with too much enthusiasm, but their legacy is not defined by how much they swilled and caroused. They left a wonderful written record of the Comstock they knew and loved. Both are inductees into the Nevada Writers Hall of Fame, and significantly, Doten's induction description includes the phrase, "[He] was a close friend and drinking companion of Dan De Quille."

3

VIOLENCE AND VIGILANTES

Virginia and Gold Hill went on a jamboree last night. If a member of the International Peace Society had been on the Comstock last night [August 21, 1876], *he would have died of a broken heart. Donnybrook paled before the reign of riot that prevailed. Fists were shot from the shoulder with utter recklessness, and pistols came from hip pockets with a frequency that causes one to marvel that the coroner has not a pile of cadavers to sit upon today.*

—*Wells Drury*

It may sound like a cliché, but Virginia City in the 1860s and 1870s had its fair share of gunfights, bar fights, murders, stage hold-ups and hangings (legally sanctioned and not). Violence and taking the law into one's own hands seemed like a way of life on the Comstock during those wild and wooly days. To be sure, later authors, such as Bernard DeVoto, Lucius Beebe and Louis L'Amour, embellished Virginia City's penchant for violence, but they were not too far off the mark. Contemporary observers, such as Dan De Quille, Mark Twain, Alf Doten and Wells Drury—all newspaper reporters and editors—left a pile of firsthand accounts that collectively attest to Virginia City's dangers. Legend has it that the first thirty graves in the Virginia City cemetery were those of men who had died by violence. Newspaper editor Wells Drury noted, "It was not unusual to see *Shot* or *Stabbed* or *Murdered* inscribed upon the tombstones and head-boards along the Comstock Lode."

One contributing factor to the violence of the place was that seemingly everyone went about town packing pistols, including the group of

Gravestone of August Bouhaben, who was murdered in Virginia City on March 31, 1892. *Courtesy of Robin Johnson.*

newspapermen mentioned. Mark Twain, in *Roughing It* (1872), said he carried a pistol because he did not want to stand out as different from the crowd. "I had never had occasion to kill anybody, nor ever felt a desire to do so, but had worn [a Colt navy revolver] in deference to popular sentiment, and in order that I might not, by its absence, be offensively conspicuous, and a subject of remark." In addition, many men wore a bowie knife in their belt, after a fashion popularized during the California gold rush.

Add alcohol, money in abundance and young men with a chip on their shoulder to the volatile mix that was Virginia City, and you have a perfect recipe for disaster. Some violence came about suddenly, after a perceived insult or accusation; tempers would flair and guns would be quickly drawn. Even Mary McNair Matthews (1880), who was not a habitué of Virginia City's saloons, knew their reputation for violence. "If they [saloon patrons] have anything to say, you generally hear it right to your face. No matter if it is good or bad, whichever party it does not suit draws a six-shooter or knife, whatever happens to be in his possession and goes for his opponent, and if he is not a dead man in five minutes, it is simply because his position does not allow him to get a good aim."

SALOON AND STREET FIGHTS

Virginia City loved a good fight. There were dog fights, cock fights, bull and bear fights (later symbolically adopted by Wall Street), boxing matches and even the occasional duel. These were clearly the days before the American Society for the Prevention of Cruelty to Animals, but the sweet science of boxing and "getting satisfaction" on the field of honor were technically against the law. However, in Virginia City, the law, such as it was, could be counted on to side with popular sentiment.

Premeditated altercations happened on occasion, such as gunslingers seeking out their rivals, but violence tended to erupt with little or no warning. The usual venue was in or near one of Virginia City's one hundred saloons. The now-cliché image of combatants tumbling out the batwing doors of a saloon was actually a regular occurrence.

For enthusiasts of the Wild West, there are some undeniable parallels between Virginia City, Nevada, and Tombstone, Arizona. Both owed their genesis as boomtowns to silver mining. They each possessed their share of saloons, gambling, prostitution and violence. While Virginia City had a greater veneer of cosmopolitan sophistication more akin to San Francisco—it did not have a Wyatt Earp or a Doc Holliday or an OK Corral—it did boast its locally notorious men.

One, Mike McGowan, had the moniker "the Man-Eater." According to Drury (1936), "Mayhem was his specialty. When aroused to cannibalistic frenzy, he sought to bite ears, nose or fingers from his antagonist." Others included Sam Brown, "Farmer" Peel and Tom Peasley. Brown was said to have killed fifteen men. Dan De Quille (1876) artfully described Brown's cocky swagger: "He walked into a saloon a side at a time, with his big Spanish spurs clanking along the floor and his six-shooter flapping under his coat-tails." When Brown picked on Carson Valley rancher Henry Van Sickle, who knew how to handle a double-barreled shotgun, his gunslinging career came to an abrupt and bloody end. Following the briefest of investigations, the coroner's jury concluded Brown's death was "a just dispensation of an all-wise providence."

An uncountable number of violent confrontations took place on the Comstock during the twenty-year boom period. Many were considered newsworthy, especially if someone died. Storey County arrest records for the period contain hundreds of assault and battery charges, the majority of which happened in the rowdier saloons of Virginia City and Gold Hill. As Alf Doten noted in 1870, "Great mania for fighting nowadays."

Sign advertising Virginia City Wild West shows. *Photograph by the author.*

One gunfight of note involved the notorious Langford "Farmer" Peel, who replaced Sam Brown as Virginia City's "cock of the walk." As often happened in the Old West, a young upstart sought to make his reputation by challenging the reigning gunslinger. In this case, it was one John Dennis, who went by the moniker "El Dorado Johnny." Johnny's decision was entirely premeditated. He put on his finest suit, got a shave and a haircut, and before seeking Peel in his habitual hangout—Lynch's Saloon on C Street—he dropped by a neighboring saloon for a little liquid courage. There, he asked the bartender, "What sort of corpse do you think I'll make?" He downed his whiskey and said, "Well, I'll be a corpse or a gentleman in less than five minutes." The subsequent gunfight in the middle of C Street resulted in the former; El Dorado Johnny was laid out on a billiard table at Lynch's, and while awaiting the undertaker, everyone admired the good-looking corpse. Incidentally, "Farmer" Peel paid for Johnny's coffin and funeral.

Comstock newspapers considered the coverage of bar fights part and parcel of their reportorial responsibility. They knew their readers had come to expect journalism's five Ws—who, what, when, where and why—in the morning paper. Occasionally, fights seemed downright comical, as when two Virginia City undertakers came to fisticuffs over the possession of a corpse in the street.

"REACH FOR THE SKY"

Some parts of Virginia City were more dangerous than others, but no place had a greater reputation for danger than "the Divide." The Divide, as its name suggests, separated the twin Comstock communities of Virginia City and Gold Hill. Topographically, it lacked distinction—a slight rise in an otherwise mountainous terrain. The Divide gained its reputation as a sparsely populated no man's land, where highwaymen would waylay their unfortunate victims, usually under the cover of darkness. Woe be the drunk stumbling through the Divide in the wee hours. Another location favored by highwaymen was Devil's Gate, a rocky cleft that separated Silver City from the mines south of Gold Hill.

Robbery victims usually survived, unscathed, depending on their willingness to cooperate. The universally understood command "reach for the sky," "hands up" or "manos arriba," was quickly followed by the brandishing of a weapon, be it Colt revolver, shotgun or bowie knife.

One incident concerning the "robbery" of Mark Twain on the Divide has been retold countless times, including an account from Twain himself. It took place on the evening of November 10, 1866, and the following is the gist of the story as recorded in Alf Doten's journal:

> *Nov. 10—Evening Mark Twain gave a lecture at Gold Hill, and on his way up here afterwards, with his Agent, Dennis E. McCarthy, on foot, they were stopped on the Divide by 5 highwaymen and robbed of about $125 in coin, and a very valuable gold watch of Mark's, worth $300....He put a card in the paper in the morning, offering to negotiate for the watch.*

> *Nov. 12—Mark Twain left on the Pioneer stage via Donner Lake route for California at noon today—Just as the stage was leaving, he being an inside passenger, a package was handed him, containing his watch, money, two jackknives, and three lead pencils which were stolen from him on the Divide, also the masks worn by the highwaymen—then, the robbers were each introduced by the names they represented that night, "Beauregard," "Stonewall Jackson," etc. Mark was considerably taken down but saw through the whole at once. He couldn't see the joke much, however, and talked to the boys quite profanely 'till the stage drove off—rather heavy on Mark. They were only trying, however, to play even on him for some of his practical jokes in former times.*

J. Ross Browne illustration, "The Devil's Gate." *Author's collection.*

Beyond the Comstock and before the completion of the V&T, people traveled by stagecoach, which came with its own risks of robbery. Highwaymen became a perennial threat in California's Gold Country beginning in the mid-1850s. Robbing passengers of their gold watches, jewelry and coin was actually ancillary to getting the strong box containing the riches of merchants and mining companies. The presence of an armed guard, called a shotgun messenger, who rode up front with the stage driver (from which we get the expression "riding shotgun"), proved little deterrent to masked outlaws.

Cheryl Anne Stapp wrote in *The Stagecoach in Northern California: Rough Rides, Gold Camps, & Daring Drivers* (2014) that stagecoaches constituted an irresistible temptation. "The very idea that a traveling stagecoach *might* be forced to surrender its treasure chest seemed to inspire a long list of the more ambitious criminally inclined." Oscar Lewis observed in *High Sierra Country* (1955) that the careers of most highwaymen were brief, and little of their biography remains for posterity. "The great majority of these, having enjoyed a few days or weeks of notoriety and come to their just rewards—usually at the end of a rope—have long since been forgotten."

The most notorious of these highwaymen was Charles E. Bowles, who was also known as Black Bart. Working alone, he successfully pulled off twenty-nine stagecoach robberies over a wide swath of California. Despite a vigorous effort to find Black Bart, he eluded his pursuers—Wells Fargo detectives and Indian trackers—for seven long years. His ultimate undoing came in 1882; it was a laundry mark on a linen handkerchief, which detectives traced to his apartment in San Francisco. Amazingly, Charles Bowles, who turned out to be an unassuming fifty-three-year-old gentleman, only served six years in San Quintin. He was released on good behavior.

Wells Fargo Express Office, 1866. *Courtesy of the Library of Congress.*

Residents of Virginia City regularly learned of stage robberies or attempted robberies from local headlines and from talk about town. To some, it was a game of cat and mouse. Stagecoach drivers, known as "Knights of the Lash," were esteemed for their nerves of steel and superhuman endurance. Men like Hank Monk became folk heroes. On the other hand, some highwaymen gained the reputations of being latter-day Robin Hoods.

One gentleman stage-robber was a man known as Nickanora, dubbed "The Spanish King." According to Drury (1936), "Nick was a many-sided personality, for he was a polished man-of-the-world as well as a debonair bandit.…He patronized the best French restaurants in Virginia City, Pioche and the other towns he favored with his visits." Another bandit with a sterling reputation was Milton Sharp. Comments from stage passengers robbed by Sharp almost sound like endorsements. "There was nothing vulgar or coarse about him. Everything was done in a business-like way, and there was no unnecessary rudeness."

Not all "road agents" had the manners and charisma of Nickanora or Sharp. In fact, most did not. It is like suggesting Captain Jack Sparrow, played so well by actor Johnny Depp, is representative of actual pirates of the Caribbean. Innocent people were killed or maimed in the course of many stagecoach robberies. For some reason, however, popular opinion seemed to make a distinction between robbing passengers and robbing treasure transported for the rich and powerful.

Stagecoaches going to and from the Comstock functioned as the 1860s equivalent of the modern armored car. Unlike the modern armored car, however, they were vulnerable, which prompted mining companies to devise a way to make theft more difficult. They switched from shipping bullion in small bars, or ingots, to shipping massive bars that were nearly impossible for a man to lift, let alone carry. Interestingly, according to Drury (1936), "many of the sports on the Comstock felt that the stratagem amounted almost to a swindle of the stage robbers who, in this instance, had the sympathy of the public."

Among the places most likely for stage holdups were the Geiger Grade, a curvy road between Virginia City and Reno, and the Bonanza Road over to Placerville, California. The latter was driver-extraordinaire Hank Monk's route. However, even Monk's fast coaches had to slow for hairpin turns on this Sierra route, and he, too, was robbed on occasion.

WARRING FACTIONS

Aside from the spontaneous bar fights and street brawls, the Comstock had some notorious battles. The Chinese population of Virginia City was divided into competing groups known as tongs, and their respective members often fought with one another. In another instance, conflicting views of who supervised a productive Comstock mine fueled violence with fatal results.

There had been a sizeable population of Chinese immigrants placer-mining the lower canyons south and east of Mount Davidson prior to the discovery of the Comstock Lode. In fact, Dayton, a community on the Carson River, was originally called "Chinatown" because of its large number of Chinese residents. In April 1859, the *Territorial Enterprise*, which was published in Genoa at the time, acknowledged the significant discovery that "[had] so long been in anticipation by the Celestials [Chinese]" was becoming reality. In keeping with the racial prejudices of the time, the European-American miners of Gold Hill immediately excluded the Chinese with the proclamation "no Chinaman shall hold a claim in this district."

Barred from direct participation in mining, the Chinese—who were first on the scene in *Yinshan* (their moniker for Nevada meaning "Silver Mountain")—as well as many others who arrived shortly thereafter, found employment in the service industries. They cooked, did laundry, cut and sold firewood and performed a host of other jobs. According to Sue Fawn Chung, the author of *In Pursuit of Gold: Chinese American Miners and Merchants in the American West* (2011), "Chinese servants were 'fashionable,' so many wealthy, prominent Comstock families had a Chinese servant or cook." Even the fictitious Cartwright family employed Hop Sing, who was played by actor Victor Sen Yung on 107 episodes of *Bonanza*. Despite their efforts to prevent Chinese people from holding lucrative or elevated positions in Virginia City, some still rose to positions of prominence, such as physicians and pharmacists who specialized in alternative and herbal medicine.

Virginia City's Chinese population also engaged in less respectable service industries: gambling, prostitution and the opium trade. In some respects, the competing Chinese organizations controlling these activities resembled what we commonly attribute to organized crime. The rival Virginia City tongs included the powerful Chinese Six Companies (also known as the Chinese Consolidated Benevolent Association), as well as the Sze Yup, the Ning Yeong and the Hop Wo Companies, among others. Most Chinese companies in Virginia City were headquartered in San Francisco.

The term "company" used to describe these Chinese groups is a little misleading, insofar as they were much more than business entities. They functioned in part like the mob, in part like a fraternal organization and in part like a labor union. Chinese companies insulated and protected their members from the frequently hostile dominant white society. While they wished to remain circumspect, given their status as a frequently reviled ethnic minority, the interactions between and among competing tongs often made headlines. Newspapers of the day reported stories with titles such as "Bloody Business in Chinatown," "Pitched Battle—Tong War" and "Murder in Chinatown." The most famous tong war in the West took place in Weaverville, California, in July 1854. Several competing tongs argued over mining rights in this Trinity County community, and when it was all over, the toll was twenty-six dead and sixty wounded.

In a situation resembling *The Godfather*, Virginia City in the mid-1870s had two rival "Dons," Sam Sing and Hop Sing. Sam Sing's headquarters were on the southeast corner of H and Union Streets, while Hop Sing's territory was three blocks away on the northwest corner of K and Union Streets. Both were fortified and bunker-like, employing sheet-iron shutters and stacks of sand-filled coal oil cans. When moving about the streets of Virginia City, both men had a retinue of heavily armed guards.

Virginia City's tong war erupted in December 1875, despite a warning from Mayor John C. Currie that hostilities in Chinatown could provoke vigilante action. Both sides even called in reinforcements from the state capital's populous Chinatown. After two months of sporadic violence, a peace treaty was finally negotiated under the direction of noted Virginia City attorney Charles De Long. It was a tenuous truce, and the rivalry persisted.

Miners on the Comstock generally performed a day's work for a day's pay and did what the superintendent directed. In one instance, a dispute over who was the rightful superintendent of the Justice Mining Company erupted into violence, which left five dead in its wake. A shootout took place over at the Waller Defeat Shaft in Gold Hill between men who were loyal to a Mr. Smith and those who backed a Mr. C.F. Kellogg, the latter having been recently selected by the mining company's board of trustees.

According to witnesses and later recounted by *Gold Hill News* editors Doten and Drury, the Waller Defeat Shafthouse was the center of the battle scene. Miners belonging to the Smith faction held this makeshift fortress at dusk on the evening of October 3, 1874, when a group led by Kellogg's brother William approached, demanding their surrender. Each side claimed to be in possession of a court order and considered themselves in the right. Unfortunately, as the group advanced, one of the Kellogg men raised a revolver, which elicited a volley from the shafthouse in response. The commotion quickly drew a crowd. The five dead men—William Kellogg, Michael Cain, John Brown, Michael Riley and W.D. Shiflett—were removed from the battle scene as a cordon surrounded the shafthouse. From their relatively secure positions behind rock and sagebrush, the men assigned to guard the little fortress were convinced the defenders would fight to the death if challenged again. Wells Drury (1936) described what they found come daylight: "In the morning, not a man was found inside the building—all had escaped, perhaps before the guard was set. A regular arsenal of shotguns and pistols was discovered, and whisky demijohns."

A coroner's inquest found all five victims had died of multiple gunshot wounds. The sheriff soon arrested four men, including one Dick Prentice, but a grand jury determined that there was insufficient evidence to charge them. Rumors persisted that Prentice, whom some called "the shotgun miner," was involved, but the affair had ended. Kellogg took over as superintendent, and men returned to the mine.

MURDERS AND HANGINGS

Homicide on the Comstock happened with an alarming frequency. Aside from the gunfights, bar fights and warring factions, the crime of murder regularly made headlines in the newspapers of Virginia City and Gold Hill. Reporters practically lived at the coroner's office and the courthouse. Aside from the two examples detailed below in which men were convicted and executed for the crime of murder, many homicides were either exonerated or remained unsolved.

That inimitable diarist and editor Alf Doten faithfully wrote in his journals about notable events that happened in Virginia City and Gold Hill. Most found longer, more detailed expression in his paper, the *Gold Hill News*, but for a capsule summary of events, the journals are unparalleled. The following is just a sampling of some Comstock murders noted by Doten:

> *Mexican murdered this evening—down on North C Street…big gash was found in left temple—no other wound. (September 16, 1865)*

> *Evening we went downtown—went to Jule Bulette's to see her body—she was foully murdered in her bed last night by some party unknown.… Worst murder ever in this city. (January 20, 1867)*

> *Cornelius A.B. Hill…found murdered…was probably killed for his money.… Detectives out after murderers—no particular clue. (April 10, 1867)*

> *Dr. Periander Pollock and wife, keeping the toll house in Six-Mile Canyon, the other side of Virginia, were murdered about 6 o'clock this evening and the house burned. (December 28, 1881)*

The most celebrated hanging ever to take place in Virginia City was that of John Millian, the man accused of murdering Julia Bulette by strangulation. After lengthy trials that went all the way to the Nevada State Supreme Court, Millian, a Frenchman who spoke little English and who maintained his innocence to the end, was hanged on April 24, 1868. To this day, there is reasonable doubt concerning his guilt or innocence.

John Millian (which was also sometimes spelled Millain or Milleain) was convicted purely on circumstantial evidence. Several months after the murder, he attempted to sell one of Julia Bulette's dresses, and that was sufficient evidence for a town that was desperate to punish the perpetrator of a heinous crime.

John Millian, the murderer of Julia Bulette. *Courtesy of the Special Collections Department, University of Nevada–Reno Libraries.*

At the time of the murder, Millian worked for Hall's Pioneer Laundry, a commercial cleaner in Virginia City. The author of this book has read the transcript of Millian's appeal to the Nevada State Supreme Court—139 pages of testimony and evidence filed on July 30, 1867. The beautiful cursive penmanship of the clerk of court, Alfred Heber, is in stark contrast to the gruesome details of the crime. The accused murderer had excellent legal representation from attorney Charles E. De Long, who spoke French, but even this nineteenth-century Perry Mason could not prove his client's innocence. It seemed his possession of Bulette's dress, even for someone who worked in a laundry and could have acquired it secondhand, was equivalent to placing him at the scene of the crime.

The Virginia City physician who examined Julia's body, Dr. Gaston, provided compelling testimony for the prosecution. "I found her lying on her back in bed with a pillow over her mouth, saturated with blood. We found two wounds upon her—one over the right eye, the other over her right temple—and also the marks of a hand upon her throat." William W. Bishop, the Storey County district attorney, emphasized how Bulette's modest house had been ransacked for valuables—fancy dresses and jewelry—and that was that. The dress became the smoking gun.

Mark Twain witnessed John Millian's public execution and wrote a piece for the *Chicago Republican* newspaper, which was published on May 31, 1868. The following is a portion of that horrific scene as described by Twain:

> *I never had witnessed an execution before, and did not believe I could be present at this one without turning away my head at the last moment. But I did not know what fascination there was about the thing, then. I only went because I thought I ought to have a lesson and because I believed that if ever it would be possible to see a man hanged, and derive satisfaction from the spectacle, this was the time….*
>
> *I watched him at that sickening moment when the sheriff was fitting the noose about his neck and pushing the knot this way and that to get it nicely adjusted to the hollow under his ear—and if they had been measuring*

> [Millian] *for a shirt, he could not have been more perfectly serene. I never saw anything like that before. My own suspense was almost unbearable—my blood was leaping through my veins, and my thoughts were crowding and trampling upon each other.*
>
> *Twenty moments to live—fifteen to live—ten to live—five—three—heaven and earth, how the time galloped!—and yet, that man stood there, unmoved, though he knew that the sheriff was reaching deliberately for the drop while the black cap descended over his quiet face!—then down through the hole in the scaffold the strap-bound figure shot like a dart!—a dreadful shiver started at the shoulders, violently convulsed the whole body all the way down and died away with a tense drawing of the toes downward, like a doubled fist—and it was over!*
>
> *I saw it all. I took exact note of every detail and even to* [Millian's] *considerately helping to fix the leather strap that bound his legs together and his quiet removal of his slippers—and I never wish to see it again. I can see that stiff, straight corpse hanging there yet, with its black pillow-cased head turned rigidly to one side, and the purple streaks creeping through the hands and driving the fleshy hue of life before them. Ugh!*

An estimated four thousand people attended John Millian's execution, including women and children. Incredibly, some even made a picnic out of the event. As James (1998) pointed out, not everyone was happy to see him hang. "Some Virginia City ladies took pity on Millian, apparently regarding his deed as not that bad. They brought him food during his stay in jail, and their kindness moved the convicted murderer to thank them from the gallows."

Virginia City witnessed another public execution, nine years after the hanging of John Millian. On January 19, 1877, Peter Larkin dropped from a scaffold behind the Storey County Courthouse. Although Alf Doten made only a cursory entry in his journal on that fateful day—"Pete Larkin was hung today at noon at Virginia for the murder of Dan Corcoran"—his trial and conviction made for sensational news. Larkin was involved in a love triangle with Barbary Coast madam Ellen "Nellie" Sayers and the murdered Daniel Corcoran, her then-lover. Nellie Sayers's saloon and brothel on South C Street did not rank high among the sporting establishments of Virginia City. Neither was Nellie Sayers held in any great esteem; the *Territorial Enterprise*, in fact, called her "the worst specimen of femininity ever to crawl down C Street." According to the court of public opinion, Sayers may have murdered Corcoran and subsequently framed her estranged lover.

At Larkin's trial, Sayers changed her testimony, first saying she had not actually witnessed Larkin shoot Corcoran to later saying she had. She attributed this contradiction to having been drunk during her first appearance on the witness stand. What may have sealed Larkin's fate was the additional testimony of Susie Brown, a fifteen-year-old prostitute in Sayers's employ. Larkin paid the price for the homicide, but community sentiment was such that Nellie Sayers left town shortly thereafter.

VIGILANTES

The West was notorious for its vigilance committees, or *vigilantes* for short, and their reputation for taking the law into their own hands. The popular Hollywood image has an angry mob lynching some unfortunate soul without the benefit of due process. Movies such as *Hang 'Em High*, the Clint Eastwood classic, or *The Ox-Bow Incident*, starring Henry Fonda and Henry Morgan, effectively convey this rush to judgement. Vigilante "justice" was meted out during the California gold rush well before the discovery of the Comstock Lode. Tens of thousands of fortune seekers inundated a fledgling San Francisco, which had limited law enforcement resources, and spread out across the Mother Lode, where miners made their own rules and punishment was swift and final.

In 1851, merchants and other law-abiding citizens of San Francisco had to contend with criminal gangs that infested the waterfront district. That district, now called the Embarcadero, went by the nickname of the Barbary Coast, a term later applied to a rowdy section of South C Street in Virginia City. Armed vigilantes hanged four men and expelled several dozen miscreants from the city. Five years later, crime and corruption had again reached epidemic proportions, necessitating vigilante intervention. Another four men were hanged but strangely with the tacit approval of city government and California governor J. Neely Johnson.

Justice in California's Gold Country in the 1850s frequently consisted of an impromptu group of miners determining the guilt or innocence of the accused. Sometimes, a saloon doubled as a courtroom, or if the crime was serious and was guilt presumed, then it was considered expedient to hold the trial beneath a tree with a stout horizontal branch. Many men met their makers in exactly this fashion, but history records the hanging of at least one woman in Downieville on July 5, 1851. Her name was Josefa Segovia, and she confessed to stabbing an assailant, Jock Cannon, through the heart. Apparently, Jock's popularity among his fellow miners, combined with a racial prejudice against Hispanics, outweighed any sensitivity the vigilantes may have felt toward the execution of a woman.

Virginia City, although violent, had comparatively little vigilante activity. The most publicized event took place in March 1871, when a group of masked men broke into the Storey County Jail and made off with a murder suspect by the name of Perkins. He was strung up on the outskirts of town. According to Drury (1936), "When the body swung clear, a fusillade of shots was fired into it." In July that same year, vigilantes hanged a man named Kirk, who did not heed an earlier warning to leave town.

There were other attempted hangings and threats of hangings on the Comstock. Alf Doten recorded a January 1868 incident in which William Conley, who killed Charles Thompson in cold blood in Gold Hill, "was arrested and taken to the county jail at Virginia for safekeeping; otherwise, he would have been lynched by the citizens." On the evening of August 24, 1873, screams from the jail in Gold Hill got the attention of neighbors, who, upon arrival, discovered a struggle between an inmate and vigilantes. Doten described the scene: "David Buffington, confined there on charge of arson, was fighting for his life in the hands of a dozen masked men who were trying to hang him—the neighborhood was alarmed by his cries, and plenty ran to the rescue, so the masked men ran away—Buffington was considerably bruised and bloody from his struggle."

After these few incidents, Virginia City vigilantes realized that the threat of violence was an effective mechanism for purging undesirables. They devised a dreaded three-digit symbol—601—which was generally understood to mean "six feet under, zero trial, one bullet or one rope." Finding a card with one's name on it and the numbers 601, a "ticket to leave," proved sufficient motivation for swift emigration.

4
KNIGHTS OF THE GREEN CLOTH

All of the pioneers who ventured into the American West of the nineteenth century were gamblers in a sense, betting on the land, the future, and themselves. They risked their fortunes and, sometimes, their very lives. And for those too impatient to wait for the bonanza of a rich ore strike, or for the cattle to multiply, or for the town to develop, the gambling table offered an opportunity for instant riches.
—Robert K. DeArment

Man is the only animal that can be skinned more than once.
—Old West adage

The title of this chapter takes its name from a book by Robert DeArment, *Knights of the Green Cloth: The Saga of the Frontier Gamblers* (1982). In the book, he argues that gambling on the western frontier was both a profession for some and a socially acceptable form of recreation for most everyone else. The green cloth, or felt, was the surface on which games of chance, most often card games, were played. The green cloth remains iconic to casino gaming tables to this day.

Virginia City was a haven for the gambler—professional and avocational alike. As Drury (1936) observed, "Everybody gambled. Even the bankers and big mining men were not excepted, their favorite retreat being the sumptuous Washoe Club, renowned for its all-night poker games." Men the likes of John Mackay and William Sharon, whose fortunes were founded on their willingness to risk it all on the Comstock mines and its infrastructure, had the reputation of being inveterate congregants around a table draped in green cloth.

During the Big Bonanza, Virginia City boasted dozens of gambling establishments, most housed within the city's thirst parlors. These variously catered to all strata of society, from the aforementioned Washoe Club for the upper crust to the one-bit saloons for the rowdier set. Not all Virginia City saloons with card games were as described by Mary McNair Matthews (1880), who doubtless never set foot in one of those dens of iniquity. "In another place, men were playing cards. A pile of money lay in the center of the table, around which four men sat playing. Each one had a revolver lying by him on the table."

The professional class of gamblers, some of whom had earlier plied their trade on Mississippi River steamboats before the Civil War disrupted that venue, included men who became quite well known in Virginia City: Hamilton Baker, Gus Botto, Jesse Bright, James "Kettle Belly" Brown, Tom Diamond, Joe Dixon, Billy Dormer, Miles Goodman, Grant Isrial, Ramon Montenegro and Joe Stewart. Some worked as dealers for gambling houses, while others were independent. Each possessed a knowledge and skill superior to the gambling public, hence their success. Joe Stewart's reputation, in fact, was such that Sharon's Bank of California would loan him money without collateral.

Most professional gamblers were men, with some notable exceptions. Eleanore Alphonsine Dumont arrived in San Francisco by way of New Orleans and eventually made her way to the California Mother Lode town of Nevada City in 1854. After checking into the National Hotel, she soon opened a gambling hall on Broad Street she called the "Vingt-Et-Un" (French for twenty-one, the popular card game also known as Blackjack). The lovely twenty-something French woman instantly became the darling of her male miner clientele.

Dumont, always the opportunist, left Nevada City for other boomtowns, and was known to have lived in the Carson City area for a time. It is said she briefly dealt Blackjack in Virginia City before moving on to mining camps in Idaho and Montana. Later in life, she was known by the sobriquet "Madame Moustache" because of the noticeable facial hair above her upper lip. Dumont ultimately settled in Bodie, California, where she died tragically by suicide on September 8, 1879.

In addition to Blackjack, which Miss Dumont so capably popularized, other games of chance one was likely to encounter in gambling palaces in Virginia City and elsewhere included draw poker, Faro, Chuck-a-luck,

High-Low and Roulette. Poker and Faro, like Blackjack, have French origins. Called *poque* in early New Orleans, poker evolved into a game dominated by bluffing and betting. Faro, sometimes known in the West as "Bucking the Tiger" because the backs of some card decks were adorned with a Bengal tiger, was all the rage in eighteenth-century France, where it went by the name Pharaon, or Pharo. Chuck-a-luck and High-Low were games played with dice. Roulette (French for little wheel), which is now synonymous with some of the world's most elegant casinos, like Monte Carlo, also had eighteenth-century roots in France and gained a huge following in western boomtowns.

The most celebrated gambling houses in Virginia City included the Delta, Gentry and Crittenden's, Pat Lynch's, the Sawdust Corner, the Sazerac and the exclusive Washoe Club. Owing to the fortunes being made in this boomtown, it was not uncommon for players at the faro and poker tables to place bets of thousands of dollars. Faro dealer Hamilton Baker once witnessed someone lay down $30,000 on the single turn of a card. These so-called whiskey and wagering emporiums generally won in the end, insofar as most games of chance were designed to favor the house.

There was an overall fondness for gambling in Virginia City, that much is certain, but the story is told how the town's wealthiest citizen, John Mackay, lost his love of poker. Michael Makley wrote in *John Mackay: Silver King in the Gilded Age* (2009), "Mackay allowed himself the diversion of poker until his wealth robbed him of its joy." He related how Mackay once said to a Comstock newspaper reporter, "Even if I win every cent in sight, it would not make a difference to me."

Poker may have lost its appeal to John Mackay, but the following story illustrates how much the game meant to the citizens of Virginia City. Although it is doubtless embellished, the story is based on a real poker game that was played in Carson City. A California newspaper, the *Argonaut*, published the story, titled "Hold the Fort," in its March 23, 1878 issue.

> *Some of the boys* [from Virginia City] *had been down to a picnic* [probably at what is now Treadway Park in Carson City], *and while there, fell into the hands of the poker Philistines. Their absence was not noticed in Virginia City, however, until about eight o'clock in the evening, when Orndorff and Magee, of the Delta, received the following dispatch:*
>
> *Send down $500 by telegraph.—Billy.*
>
> *Then, it was known that Billy Robinson and some of the boys were down at Carson, holding the fort for reinforcements. The Delta boys, with*

Poker players. *Courtesy of the Special Collections Department, University of Nevada–Reno Libraries.*

characteristic promptness, sent the required sum and waited anxiously for the next hour, when they received the following:

Send $1,000 more and Joe Dixon.—Billy.

Dixon was soon found.... The situation was at once explained....

It was a little before midnight when the horses, drenched with foam, reached the city. There was no time to lose. They began to hunt the leading sporting resorts and soon found Billy Robinson and his gang in the hands of a crowd, whom the newcomers recognized, at a glance, as the very flower of paste-board chivalry of Carson.

Joe is an open-up sort of a man and, walking up to the table, remarked: "I s'pose a man with coin can take a hand here?" And he laid down his bag.

Nothing suited the Carson chaps better...and a fresh deal inaugurated as they took the places of the Virginia men, who had been fighting, like the soldiers of Marathon in the Pass of Thermopylae, since noon.

Meanwhile, the Delta Saloon in Virginia City was the scene of an anxious gathering, and the bulletins from the seat of war were posted up.... Won $360. Bluffed $700. Lost $1,500. Send down more coin. [The Delta authorized $10,000 by telegraph.]

> *At a little after 3 o'clock, Huntley* [another Virginia City sharp] *stalked in. He showed the requisite amount of coin, and the Carsonites laughed inwardly because they had another victim. He looked like a divinity student. When he dealt, his thin hands played like lightening over the pack; his shuffle was the work of a magician, and the cards seemed alive.*
>
> [Hours later, a massive pot was on the table; winner take all, which is exactly what the Virginia City poker players did.]
>
> *The morning light was stealing in just as the worsted Carson gamesters were stealing out.... "What did you have?" asked Joe. "Don't know," said Mr. Huntley. "To tell you the truth, I haven't yet looked at my hand. If a man looks at his hand, sometimes he gets confused and loses his nerve."*

CHEATING AND ITS CONSEQUENCES

Not all card games ended peacefully. One of the cardinal sins on the western frontier was cheating at cards; it ranked just below horse theft and was considered a capital offense. The accusation of cheating would quickly escalate the conversation to the next level, which often involved violence. Mary McNair Matthews's description of men at a poker table with revolvers at the ready had some basis in fact. Judging from reports in the local press, such as the following excerpt from the *Territorial Enterprise* (March 23, 1867), disputes over card games were not uncommon.

> *BELLIGERENT—Last evening, two gentlemen, who held different opinions in regard to some matter connected with a game of cards, being unable through the medium of words, agreed to decide the point in dispute by means of the more forcible argument of blows. It was agreed to hold the debate outside of the city limits, where no officer of the law would be likely to interfere with the harmony of the discussion.*

Cheating was widespread in the West, and Virginia City was not immune. According to Robert DeArment, "Wherever there is gambling, there will be found the crooked gambler; wherever a game of chance is played with money to be wagered, there will appear those who would eliminate the element of chance." Every sharp had multiple cheating skills in their repertoires—sleight-of-hand, marked cards, loaded dice and rigged roulette wheels. Some so-called games of chance had a notorious reputation—the worst being the three shells and pea, and its card game variant, three-card monte.

Among the popular card games, poker had the greatest potential for manipulation by sharps. Both Blackjack and Faro had designated house dealers, and players had minimal contact with the cards. Assuming a game had an honest dealer and a fresh deck, opportunities to mark cards were limited. Poker, on the other hand, allowed ample opportunity for players to mark cards. According to Oscar Lewis, the author of *Sagebrush Casinos: The Story of Legal Gambling in Nevada* (1953), various card marking methods included "bending one corner or making a tiny dent in its edge" or "contriving to make telltale smears or smudges on their backs that to other players—if they [noticed] them at all—[would] appear to be the result of ordinary use."

Crooked dealers also had a plethora of techniques at their disposal. One consisted of trimming the edges of a deck, whereby certain cards, aces for example, were slightly wider and could be manipulated by nimble fingers. These high-value cards could be shifted to the bottom of the deck to be dealt selectively, usually with a winning effect. In western saloon culture, to accuse someone of "dealing from the bottom of the deck" was the same as calling him a cheat.

In a society where most men went about armed, a declaration of cheating constituted a challenge that was most often met with weapons drawn, if not fired. One such incident took place on a stagecoach traveling from Salt Lake City to Virginia City. The four passengers—Bill Ayers, Mike Conoley, Joe Goddard and Gaspard LeCoeur—all professional gamblers, naturally passed the time in a friendly game of draw poker. According to Bill Graves, the stagecoach driver, he heard a barrage of gunfire from within the coach just as they were approaching Gold Canyon. He pulled to a stop and jumped down to investigate. Ayers, Conoley and Goddard were dead, and LeCoeur, although still alive, was "well-ventilated." Apparently, the accusation of cheating had been made and was met with unfortunate consequences.

Other Gambling

Other gambling took place farther down the slope of Mount Davidson. Virginia City's Chinatown contained many gambling halls that catered to its Chinese residents and to whites who wanted try their luck among the "celestials." Chinese immigrants in the Far West (sometimes called celestials for the "Celestial Empire," one of the names for China) were passionate about gambling. It was more than socially acceptable; a successful Chinese gambler was a revered figure within the community. The 1870 U.S. decennial census for Virginia City, in fact, identified forty-two men in Chinatown whose profession was listed as "gambler."

Games of chance that could be found in Chinatown included, of course, various forms of poker, but the most popular games were uniquely Chinese. Among these were Fan-Tan and several forms of the lottery. Fan-Tan was a game of considerable antiquity, dating back at least two thousand years in China. It was fundamentally a game of division, whereby a square on a table was divided into four sections, labeled one through four; players placed bets on how many gambling pieces—small coins, beans, buttons or tokens—would remain after the banker dumped several handfuls of the gambling pieces on the table and then removed them four at a time, using a bamboo stick. Ultimately, four or fewer pieces would remain, and winners who placed their bets on the remaining number were paid by the banker at a rate triple their bet.

Fan-Tan gambling pieces can still be found throughout Nevada and California in archaeological sites where Chinese immigrants once resided. In his book *Virginia City: Secrets of a Western Past* (2012), Ronald James described *chu* pieces—"round, black and white, hemispherical dollops of glass"—which have been found on the Comstock and elsewhere. The Chinese also used *wen* coins, whose monetary value was negligible. Sites associated with railroad construction, woodcutter camps in the Sierra and Chinatowns on the mining frontier contain these gambling pieces, mixed in with other artifacts of Chinese material culture—celadon rice bowls, soy sauce jars and opium-smoking paraphernalia. Another popular game of chance played in Virginia City's Chinatown was a lottery game *bak gop biu* ("white pigeon ticket"), known today as the popular casino game of Keno. At some point in the nineteenth century, numbers replaced Chinese characters on the lottery cards, but the game is essentially the same.

Like the Chinese, the local Paiutes in Virginia City, whose amorphous settlement was located down Six Mile Canyon, loved to gamble. Unlike the Chinese, however, their games were played only among themselves, and they did not utilize any designated gambling houses. Small groups were commonly seen sitting in circles outdoors, huddled over a modern deck of playing cards or an indigenous game of chance.

Regardless of the game of chance played, the sums wagered or the ethnicity of participants, Virginia City residents loved to gamble. It was their passion, their pastime and, for some, their profession.

5

CYPRIANS AND NYMPHS OF THE PAVE

The rich vocabulary applied to Comstock prostitution suggests its size and importance in the community, and thirteen different words for prostitution were used regularly in newspaper stories and contemporary commentaries. While some of those words reflected a Victorian penchant for euphemisms and reporters' attempts to pepper their writing with arresting terms, the large number of synonyms for prostitute also indicates the centrality of commercial sex to people on the Lode. Some phrases which were synonymous with the word "prostitute" implied general conceptions about commercial sex. Thus "soiled dove" and "fair but frail" communicated the idea that prostitutes were fragile creatures who had fallen into sin. On the other hand, "woman of the town," "woman of easy virtue," and "woman of ill repute" indicated the promiscuous, public nature of prostitutes' sexuality.
—Marion S. Goldman

In addition to those identified by Marion Goldman in the epigraph above, other synonyms for prostitute in common usage on the Comstock were courtesan, harlot, whore, Cyprian (Homer's term for Aphrodite, the Greek goddess of love) and nymph du pave. Two other terms—keeper of a hotel de refreshment and madam—were associated with women who operated a brothel. Although some of these terms may be antiquated and unknown today, they were part of vernacular speech and print in the nineteenth century, as exemplified by this March 21, 1867 piece in the *Territorial Enterprise*: "CYPRIANS ARRESTED—Three 'nymphs of the pave' were yesterday taken into custody by the police, for disorderly conduct at the Tahoe House and will have a hearing in the recorder's court this morning."

Although confined to certain precincts—a slight nod to Victorian morality—sexual commerce was both legal and popular. Even if one avoided walking past the Barbary Coast on South C Street, which took its name from the infamous San Francisco red-light district, or the line of cribs and brothels on D Street, prostitution was impossible to ignore. Often identifiable by their flamboyant attire, prostitutes shopped, attended the opera and otherwise went about town in a very visible manner, which, in fact, could be considered a form of advertising. People read about them in the newspapers with some frequency. And one prostitute, Julia Bulette, even enjoyed the status of honorary membership in the Virginia City Fire Engine Company No. 1. Even out-of-town visitors who arrived in Virginia City by train could not avoid an awareness of prostitution. The D Street red-light district lay squarely between the V&T Railroad Station and commercial C Street. Detraining passengers often remarked that the sight of a brothel meant "Welcome to Virginia City!"

Virginia City Red-Light District plaque, D Street. *Courtesy of Robin Johnson.*

Prostitutes comprised such a large percentage of women in the early years of the Comstock Lode that single women, like Mary McNair Matthews, worried she would be mistaken for one. She operated a Virginia City boardinghouse in the 1870s and kept another woman among her otherwise all-male boarders for the sake of appearances. Matthews (1880) explained her reasoning:

> *My minister said to me one day, when I was telling him how hard it was to have to board and lodge one person for nothing in order to keep from being talked about (for I always regarded my character as the apple of my eye): "Let them talk; they do not buy your bread and butter. Do what conscience tells you is right, and let them talk if they choose."*

PROSTITUTION'S SOCIAL HIERARCHY

Not all Virginia City prostitutes were equal. They had, of course, the common denominator of engaging in sexual commerce, but their lifestyles could be worlds apart—from the elegant courtesan of a mining magnate, for instance, to the enslaved Chinese prostitute. According to Jacqueline Baker Barnhart in *The Fair but Frail: Prostitution in San Francisco, 1849–1900* (1986), "The status of prostitutes was defined by their clientele and the environment in which they worked and lived." Perhaps nowhere else was a hierarchy among prostitutes more evident than in New Orleans, arguably the most sinful city in nineteenth-century America. Troy Taylor wrote in *Wicked New Orleans: The Dark Side of the Big Easy* (2010) that this infamous city offered everything "from the expensive parlor house to the fifteen-cent crib."

In *Gold Diggers and Silver Miners: Prostitution and Social Life on the Comstock Lode* (1981), Marion Goldman elaborates on the social hierarchy of prostitution in Virginia City, which was not unlike that of San Francisco. "In general terms, there were elite, middle-, working- and lower-class prostitutes, as well as madams and saloonkeepers [pimps] who remained essentially outside of active prostitution."

The elite prostitutes lived by their wits and charm and often became the mistresses of wealthy men. Bonanza King and U.S. senator James Fair kept women in San Francisco, Virginia City and in our nation's capital, leading his wife to eventually sue for divorce on the grounds of "habitual adultery."

Jacqueline Barnhart (1986) cited the example of one elite prostitute in San Francisco who earned $50,000 in one year and retired. Many elite prostitutes remained low-profile, not needing to publicize their profession, but others embraced a life in the public eye. Some elite prostitutes were "actresses" who made themselves available to select clients while touring American and European cities.

Middle-class prostitutes enjoyed a certain degree of self-sufficiency and were either independent contractors or worked in one of Virginia City's more elegant brothels, such as Cad Thompson's "Brick" or Jenny Tyler's "Bow Windows." They generally developed a select clientele and could afford to pick and choose with whom to share their sexual favors. Julia Bulette and Rosa May belonged to this middle-class group of courtesans on the Comstock; they did well by the standards of their profession but never matched the wealth acquired by the elites. For example, Julia Bulette (who is discussed in another chapter of this book) lived in a small two-room cottage on D Street, not, as Susan James pointed out in her *Nevada Magazine* article about Bulette cleverly titled "Queen of Tarts" (1984), the legendary "palace" ascribed to her years later.

The majority of those who engaged in sexual commerce in Virginia City were working-class prostitutes, according to Goldman's (1981) hierarchy. Unlike middle-class prostitutes, they could not afford to be choosey and usually entertained sequential partners during their "shift." They solicited in the bit saloons and populated the cheaper brothels. Their income, which was estimated to be one dollar per customer, offered a subsistence wage, provided they did not succumb to an addiction to drugs or alcohol, which seemed an occupational hazard.

Finally, lower-class prostitutes included Asian women who were essentially kept as slaves in Chinatown cribs. According to the dictates of their culture, Chinese men regulated sexual commerce and received all profits. San Francisco, the center of Chinese immigration on the West Coast, functioned as a slave market, where women were bought and sold as chattel. According to a local census taken in 1875, Virginia City housed seventy-five Chinese prostitutes. Lower-class prostitutes also included "slatterns" and "vagrants," who eked out a living on the streets of Virginia City. These women often had severe substance abuse problems and could not hold a regular job—in a brothel or elsewhere. Goldman (1981) cited the example of one woman who personified this group: "Mary Ramshart was the most persistent and problematic prostitute-vagrant on the Comstock because of her vulgar public behavior and her many illegitimate children."

Mary, Susie and Nellie, Chinese wives who were often misidentified as prostitutes, 1866. *Courtesy of the Special Collections Department, University of Nevada–Reno Libraries.*

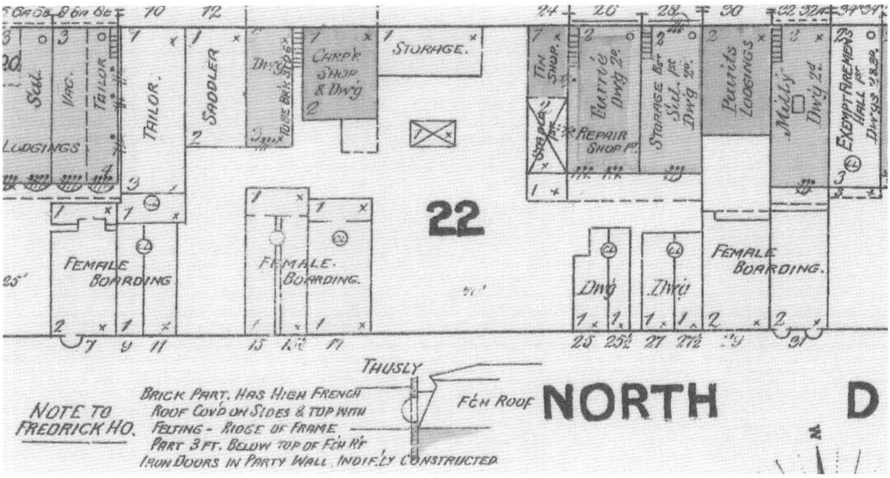

A portion of a Sanborn Fire Insurance map that shows D Street brothels labeled as "Female Boarding," 1890. *Courtesy of the Special Collections Department, University of Nevada-Reno Libraries.*

Virginia City cribs, D Street, 1924. *Courtesy of the Special Collections Department, University of Nevada–Reno Libraries.*

Buildings exclusively devoted to prostitution went by various names. One euphemism employed by city mapmakers, such as the Sanborn Fire Insurance Company, was "female boarding." Other terms—brothel, parlor house and crib—were less ambiguous. Jacqueline Barnhart (1986) explained that, in the nineteenth century, these conveyed a sense of both functionality and hierarchy.

> *Brothel, of course, designated any house of prostitution. A parlor house, though, was the elite location where graciousness and decorum were maintained. A crib was the most degraded kind of house. It was usually built exclusively for prostitution and consisted of numerous small (six-by-eight-foot) rooms all opening onto the street by door or window, allowing the prostitute to attract customers.*

Virginia City had them all, especially in the D Street red-light district. Interestingly, a group of cribs, sometimes referred to as "Sporting Row," survived along D Street as part of the urban landscape well into the twentieth century.

A Mistress, a Madam and a Prostitute

Boomtown Virginia City was a great place for commercial sex. The town contained a large population of single men—and married men who behaved as if they were single. They had money to spend. Women who parlayed sex for money were drawn like moths to a flame.

The following are three vignettes of Comstock Cyprians of note. Prior to introducing them, however, a few definitions are needed, in accordance with Jacqueline Barnhart's (1986) work on the subject. She defined a *mistress* as "the illicit ladylove of a married man [and]...a prostitute only if her motives were known to be financial." Although considered a term of polite respect, when used within the context of prostitution, a *madam* was someone who "ran the elite parlor houses and better-class brothels." The generic term for prostitute—*whore*—almost always conveyed a pejorative meaning.

Laura Fair

One Comstock mistress who could not avoid the public eye was Laura D. Fair (unrelated to Bonanza King James Fair). Laura Fair (maiden name unknown) was born in Holly Springs, Mississippi, in 1837 and married a New Orleans merchant at the age of sixteen. After his death and a second unsuccessful marriage, Laura moved to San Francisco, where she and her mother operated a boardinghouse. She met and married attorney William D. Fair in Shasta, California, but after his suicide three years later, Laura, her mother and Laura's young daughter from her third marriage found themselves desperate to make a living in expensive San Francisco.

According to Goldman (1981), "Laura had no assets other than her looks and charm, so she went on stage and appeared opposite Junius Brutus Booth in a benefit performance of Sheridan's *School for Scandal*. The San Francisco benefit netted her enough money to pay her debts and rent a lodging house in Virginia City." Among the lodgers at Fair's Tahoe House on South C Street, which opened in September 1862, was a married man by the name of Alexander P. Crittenden.

Crittenden, an attorney from San Francisco who was then making a pile of money from Comstock mining litigation, took Fair, his landlady, as a mistress. Thus began their seven-year affair. Crittenden lavished his mistress with expensive gifts, money and the promise of marriage once he divorced his present wife—or so he said. Eventually, Fair was fed up with being kept on tenterhooks, and on November 3, 1870, she confronted Crittenden aboard a ferry in San Francisco Bay. The woman pulled out a pistol and shot her lover in the chest at point-blank range.

Laura Fair was arrested immediately and charged with murder. Two of the most celebrated suffragists of the day, Susan B. Anthony and Elizabeth Cady Stanton, paid a visit to Fair in her jail cell while she awaited trial, which suggested their sympathy for the defendant. The trial in San Francisco was a complicated one, with arguments about the nature of a woman's role in an adulterous affair, "female hysteria" and crimes of passion, but ultimately, she was convicted and scheduled for execution. Laura's attorney managed to get a new trial on appeal, and that resulted in the murder charge being overturned. Amazingly, Laura Fair got away with murder, but public sentiment back on the Comstock was not on her side, as expressed in this *Gold Hill News* opinion piece: "The she-devil, Mrs. Fair, who kept the Tahoe House…deserved hanging long ago." Laura Fair died in San Francisco in 1919 in relative anonymity.

Laura D. Fair. *Courtesy of the Special Collections Department, University of Nevada–Reno Libraries.*

Cad Thompson

Probably the most well-known madam on the Comstock was Caroline "Cad" Thompson, who was born Sarah Hagen in Ireland in 1827. Thompson immigrated to America as a young widow with her five-year-old son, Henry, in tow, and in the mid-1860s, she found herself in the boomtown of Virginia City. In *Wicked Women: Notorious, Mischievous, and Wayward Ladies of the Old West* (2015), Chris Enss wrote, "Cad was a shrewd businesswoman who determined early on that she could capitalize on the lustful miners' need for women. She purchased a large, two-story brick house, moved five attractive ladies in, and invited the public to one of the town's most elegant parlor houses."

Cad Thompson's popular-but-pricey brothel became known simply as the "Brick," a moniker often applied to Thompson herself. The Brick, situated at 56 North D Street, near the corner of Sutton Avenue, had a good reputation during its many years of operation; there were no prostitute suicides there, and among the few customers who were shot, only one died.

The layout of the Brick was probably typical of the more elegant brothels of the era. The "working women" lived in the basement. The first floor contained two parlors that were furnished with lace curtains, chandeliers, a plush carpet and comfortable sofas and chairs. The parlors exemplified Victorian décor and provided a convivial place in which to negotiate the business of commercial sex under the watchful eye of Madam Thompson. The actual transaction took place upstairs in one of the five bedrooms.

Cad Thompson was reputed to have a fiery temper, which some attributed to her Irish heritage. At least twice, her fighting disposition created a sensation in Virginia City. She and her lover, fellow Irishman John Dalton, were famous for their violent quarrels, and during one spat at the Brick on July 4, 1867, a police officer arrived just as Dalton was pointing a derringer toward Thompson's breast. The officer shot and killed him on the spot.

Another violent incident involved Thompson and one of her prostitutes, Mary Livingston. The two got into an argument that turned physical, and the madam beat Mary to within an inch of her life. Livingston subsequently charged her employer with assault and battery. Although Thompson was acquitted—such was Virginia City's frontier justice—some members of the community sided with Livingston and took justice into their own hands.

In the early morning hours of November 18, 1866, some of those who sympathized with Mary Livingston showed up outside the Brick. They set fire to some straw bales in front of the house, and the fire spread rapidly to the Brick itself. The arsonists eventually put the fire out with a fire company engine they had conveniently brought along with them. Alf Doten, a frequent Brick customer, made the following entry in his journal:

> *Some fellows took No. 1's engine about 4 o'clock this morning and washed out old Cad Thompson's whore house—Gave her hell—created quite a consternation among the law and order portion of the Community—not the end of it yet—we shall have to see who rules the city now, the roughs or decent men.*

Doten evidently included himself in the latter group—decent men who did not wish to see their favorite brothel—and favorite madam—treated in such a mean-spirited way. Undeterred, Cad rebuilt the severely damaged Brick and built two other houses of prostitution for good measure.

Cad Thompson moved to San Francisco in 1880, although she continued to own the Brick until 1892. The mining bonanza on the Comstock had begun to turn to *borrasca* (a Spanish word for mining depression), and business was down. Besides, her son, Henry, had committed suicide in 1878 at the age of twenty-two by shooting himself in the chest with a pistol. Despite the turmoil that surrounded Cad Thompson, the Brick—the house and its madam—became a significant part of the legacy of prostitution in Virginia City. Cad Thompson's ultimate fate is unknown, but it is assumed she died and was buried in San Francisco.

Rosa May

Born Rosa Elizabeth White in 1855, Rosa May left an unhappy home in Pennsylvania at the age of sixteen and moved to New York City, where she became a prostitute. A few years later, May migrated to various Western mining boomtowns before arriving in Virginia City in 1875; there, she worked in Cad Thompson's parlor house, the Brick. Rosa May was young and attractive and quickly became the toast of the town.

May and Thompson became good friends, in spite of Madam Thompson's difficult demeanor. She worked at the Brick, as well as one of Thompson's other brothels at 18 South D Street. Thompson must have trusted her star prostitute because May sometimes managed the business in Virginia City when her employer was in San Francisco. In a letter dated March 27, 1880,

Rosa May. *Author's collection.*

that was mailed from San Francisco, Cad began with the salutation "Friend Rosa," an indication that May was more than a trusted subordinate.

Like many of the prostitutes who worked the line in Virginia City, Rosa May also went down to the state capital on occasion. Extra help was needed when the state legislature was in session, so madams Emma Goldsmith, Jennie Moore and Mary Ann Phillips would call up to Virginia City for reinforcements. Carson's red-light district was situated along Ormsby Street (now Curry), between Second and Fifth Streets, which meant that several celebrated parlor houses were only a short walk from the state capitol building.

There is more known about the life of Rosa May than any other Virginia City prostitute (with the possible exception of Julia Bulette). George Williams III pieced together her biography in *Rosa May: The Search for a Mining Camp Legend* (1979), a first-person narrative detailing his obsession with May. A significant part of the book includes twenty-five previously unpublished letters that were found in a trunk belonging to Rosa May that was bought at auction in 1934. This correspondence, written by eight people, including one by Cad Thompson, spans the period September 27, 1876, and March 27, 1880.

From the Rosa May letters, we learn, for example, that she had a romantic relationship with a Gold Hill man who went by the name of Ernest Marks. Marks was obviously smitten, beginning his letters with salutations such as "My Own Darling" and concluding them with "Sweet Kisses" and the like. Although the collection only contains one side of the correspondence between Marks and May, his letters to her indicate that the romance was reciprocated. His letter to May dated February 15, 1879, begins, "Your dear kind and loving letter I am in receipt of today. Thank you, darling, for being so prompt in answering my letters." The fact that May kept these letters in her trunk for years afterward is itself testimony of their relationship.

A couple of the letters, more notes because of their brevity, are clearly business related. One from Rosa May to someone named Leo dated August 18, 1879, reads, "Having arrived in town, again I write to inform you of my address, and if you wish to call and see me, I would be pleased to have you do so. I am living with Mrs. C. Thompson." It is the only letter in the collection from May in her own hand because it was returned to the sender. Another letter is from Isaac Isaacs, one of Rosa May's regulars who owned a clothing store on South C Street. It reads, "Miss Rosa. Please come to my room tonight. If you wish, come between 9 and 10. The front door will be open, so walk right in to my room, and I will be on up as soon as I close the store." Apparently, May would make house calls for preferred customers like Mr. Isaacs.

Rosa May's tenure as a Virginia City prostitute came to an end with the closing of the Brick in 1892. At that time, the mining town of Bodie, California, was booming, so May, although she was in her late thirties at the time, continued to ply her trade among the miners. She was not alone in moving to Bodie; her friend and former Carson City madam Emma Goldsmith was there. Significantly, so was her Comstock lover, Ernest Marks. According to Williams (1979), "From '93 until her death [in 1912], Rosa and Marks had a steady relationship."

Rosa May died during a virulent outbreak of pneumonia while tending to stricken miners, according to Ella Cain in *The Story of Bodie* (1956). Although the story of her nursing the sick until she herself succumbed has not been corroborated, it would not have been out of character. The "whore with the heart of gold" may be apocryphal, but it is entirely possible Rosa May was merciful as well as mercenary. She was buried in the Bodie Cemetery.

THE DARK SIDE

Prostitute Suicide

The commercial sex trade took its toll. The life of a prostitute, especially those among the lower ranks, could be physically and psychologically punishing. Aside from the risks of sexually transmitted diseases, unwanted pregnancy and abusive customers, one commonplace occupational hazard was substance abuse. Most prostitutes drank, and many used drugs, such as the opium derivative laudanum. Tragically, drug overdose—whether intentional or accidental—was the cause of death for more than a few prostitutes. In fact, the suicide of a prostitute in Virginia City hardly made the news. Papers like the *Territorial Enterprise* would run a line or two in the "Local Matters" column, almost as an aside and rarely with an expression of sympathy.

Alf Doten, who knew Virginia City's brothels and their women as well as anyone, wrote in his journal on February 6, 1868, about the suicide of prostitute Ida Vernon. His account reads more like a police report than a diary entry about a woman with whom he had been intimate.

> *Little Ida, that I used to* [erasure] *some 2 yrs ago was found dead in her bed at the "Bow Windows" (Jenny Tyler's) this morning—she has been rather dissipated for some time past and latterly had taken to opium—Ida Vernon was her name—about 32 yrs old—a man was sleeping with her and found her cold in the morning—rest in peace Ida—she was her worst enemy.*

Local opinion considered Ida Vernon's case noteworthy from the perspective of the man who had woken up next to a dead prostitute. It seems his shock carried more weight than her death.

The more than forty prostitute suicides or attempts that received remark in local papers included that of Nellie Davis, who lived on B Street and died of a morphine overdose; Clara Howard, a D Street prostitute who shot herself; and Frankie Norton, who made multiple attempts to kill herself by overdosing on laudanum. One of Frankie's attempts was thwarted by a doctor who pumped her stomach, and once revived, she angrily vowed to try again. Blanche De Maude acquired the nickname "Suicide Frenchy" because of her many unsuccessful attempts to end her life.

Goldman (1981) discussed one dimension of prostitute suicide in purely economic terms. There were cases in which a homemade emetic consisting of mustard and olive oil would be given to prostitutes who drank poison. She argued that attempts to save the victim could be ascribed to self-serving reasons, insofar as "death in a brothel would probably slow business for several days." As callous as that may seem, a group mentality may have been a greater consideration than the welfare of the individual.

On the other hand, women in Virginia City brothels sometimes made suicide pacts. Goldman (1981) cited two examples:

> *Two sets of prostitutes made pacts in the summer of 1872, and the earlier suicide might have been a model for the later attempt. In July of that year, two fashionably dressed young women were found dead in a solitary cabin on B Street. Their names were not mentioned in the newspaper, but the article noted that their skins had the "rosy hue" of arsenic eaters. About five weeks later, another suicide pact caused a far greater uproar—in part because it had a "happy" ending, and the two prostitutes survived.*

As one can imagine, a prostitute's life in Chinatown must have been miserable. These women were bought, sold and kept as slaves. During the years of the Comstock boom, six Chinese prostitutes chose suicide as a means of escape.

THE DEMISE OF BARBARY COAST

By 1877, there began a hue and cry to clean up the Barbary Coast. After all, C Street was the main thoroughfare of Virginia City, and this notorious red-light district, located between Flowery and Silver Streets, was impossible to miss. Two factors contributed to this change: the great fire of 1875 and the opening of the Fourth Ward School the following year.

The 1875 fire was the most devastating in Virginia City's history; it destroyed most of the town—from two blocks above A Street to five blocks below D Street and between Taylor and Carson Streets. The conflagration totally disrupted prostitution along the charred remains of D Street. Ronald James (1998) explained, "The Coast became even more of a haven for Virginia City's prostitutes and toughs. Although the area had a reputation for attracting the darker elements of society, the fire exacerbated the problem with refugees, making the intrusion on C Street all the more noticeable."

Fourth Ward School, 1940. *Photograph by Arthur Rothstein. Courtesy of the Library of Congress.*

More alarming to the growing number of Virginia City families was the proximity of the Barbary Coast to the newly constructed Fourth Ward School at 537 South C Street. Parents protested and told city officials that their children should not have to "run the gauntlet" to and from school every day.

Numerous newspaper exposés revealed the extent to which prostitution held sway and influence in Virginia City. John Piper, for one, came under scrutiny. As the owner of the popular Piper's Opera House and as a former mayor, he was a pillar of the community. More telling, however, was his status as a state senator and his service as a chairman of the Senate Committee on Public Morals. Piper received criticism for his attempts to block legislation restricting the location of brothels in town while, at the same time, owning brothel property in the Barbary Coast neighborhood, an apparent conflict of interest.

Public opinion prevailed in a campaign to clean up the Barbary Coast. According to Goldman (1981), "Citizens' complaints finally led to three saloonkeepers' convictions for disorderly conduct, and by the summer of 1877, respectable businesses had replaced almost all of the saloons on the Coast." A few prostitutes continued to conduct business on the Barbary Coast in the 1880s, but by then, the Big Bonanza had ended, and many miners and "camp followers" had left for other boomtowns. Prostitution remained legal in Virginia City until 1949, when the brothel business shifted to the northern part of Storey County, morphing into the famous Mustang Ranch.

6

THE FRENCH CONNECTION

That is the Can-can. The idea of it is to dance as wildly, as noisily, as furiously as you can; expose yourself as much as possible....I suppose French morality is not of that strait-laced description which is shocked at trifles.
—Mark Twain

Virginia City had a love affair with the French—call it Francophilia, if you prefer. The finest cuisine was French, the most sought-after prostitutes were French and French was the language of love. This love affair included, of course, Paris—*La Ville Lumière*—and, by extension, New Orleans. In fact, the capital city of the old Louisiana colony, which became part of the United States in 1803, had acquired quite a reputation long before the discovery of gold in California or silver in Nevada.

The French joie de vivre found fertile ground on the Comstock. It provided a welcome contrast to a forbidding landscape, harsh climate and dangerous and difficult work. There was a welcome release in celebrating life à la française rather than in accordance to the nose-to-the-grindstone Protestant work ethic. It is no wonder, therefore, that Adah Isaacs Menken and Julia Bulette, a New Orleans entertainer and a prostitute, respectively, found Virginia City so congenial. They personified a credo that was heard frequently in bayou land, *laissez les bons temps rouler*—let the good times roll.

Interestingly, this relationship was a two-way street. More than a few who made a pile of money on the Comstock chose to spend it in

Paris, including "Sandy" and Eilley Orrum Bowers, the Comstock's first millionaires, and Marie Louise Hungerford Mackay, the wife of Bonanza king John Mackay. Mrs. Mackay actually moved to Paris, living there from 1876 to 1884, while her miner-millionaire husband kept her in a lifestyle to which she became accustomed.

French culture thrived in Virginia City; it was a mosaic of the foreign-born, each contributing to the cosmopolitan milieu, like Monsieur Chavel, who taught fencing to Mark Twain and Dan De Quille. The most elegant hotel in town, the International, boasted a French cook and baker, and Alf Doten's journals from the Big Bonanza years documented his frequent dining at Chaumond's French Rotisserie on C Street. Doten also noted how the French celebrated Bastille Day (July 14) "with a procession—4th of July style."

Members of the medical profession in Virginia City included Frenchmen—Drs. Lasvignes, Desch and Lefevre. Although all three doctors advertised their services, Dr. Jean Baptiste B. Lefevre achieved the greatest notoriety. Dr. Lefevre moved to Virginia City in 1868 and owned the French Drugstore on 204 South C Street. He billed himself as a physician, surgeon and *accoucheur* (the French term for a male obstetrician). Fundamentally, he was the doctor to Virginia City's prostitute population. Dan De Quille noted that Dr. Lefevre capitalized on his Parisian origin, saying that everyone loved his distinct French accent.

Wells Drury (1936) recognized that this Francophilia existed in much of the rest of Nevada as well. His short poem, titled *Nevada Dancers*, paid homage to the love of dance and echoed Mark Twain's fascination with the can-can.

Nevada's the boss state for dancers,
And all modern choice social games;
The folks, young and old, are all prancers,
And give their clubs high Frenchy names.

Virginia sports the Entre Nous,
While Reno boasts the Bien Vue;
Elko has the Comme il Faut,
In such things Austin's A Propos.

The Carsons claim the gay Au Fait,
In Silver 'tis the Coup d'Essai;
Aurora folks meet En Ami,
And Pioche gets the Coup de Pied.

Then come to Nevada for dancing,
If you do, you'll see lots of fun;
The music and girls are enticing—
As fine as you'll find 'neath the sun.

This chapter explores the seamier side of French culture as it manifested itself in Virginia City. As an adjective, the word *seamy* implies a value judgment, its synonyms being *sordid* and *disreputable*. Virginia City, however, reveled in its many pleasures and never aspired to become a bastion of morality. As Well Drury (1936) put it, "In the effete eastern states, a man would be sent to jail for doing those things which serve to daily and nightly amuse the Nevada gentleman. Thus, it is seen how the mind broadens in its views as it travels west."

VIVE LA DIFFÉRENCE

According to Goldman (1981), "On the West Coast, French prostitutes had a special reputation for mysterious fast living that added to their allure." Curt Gentry, in his book *The Madams of San Francisco* (1964), cited this observation of a gold rush–era resident of the City by the Bay. "Americans were irresistibly attracted by their graceful walk, their supple and easy bearing and charming freedom of manner, qualities, after all, only found in France; and they trooped after a French woman whenever she put her nose out of doors, as if they could never see enough of her."

This placing of French women, particularly those of easy virtue, on a pedestal certainly took place in Virginia City. In their chapter in *Comstock Women* (1998) titled "Women of the Mining West: Virginia City Revisited," Ronald James and Kenneth Fliess added that some Virginia City prostitutes passed themselves off as French in order to increase their appeal. "Euro-Americans were often the preferred prostitutes on the Comstock, but those who professed French nativity could most easily strive for higher status."

Not all French prostitutes—real or imagined—were happy with their lots in life. Blanche de Maude, who worked in Bow Windows, a famous brothel in Virginia City's Barbary Coast, acquired the nickname "Suicide Frenchy" because she had twice attempted to take her own life. Thanks to the swift intervention of a doctor, both attempts were unsuccessful. No one knows if that moniker subsequently affected her trade, but given Virginia

French actresses dressed for a mine tour. *Courtesy of the Nevada Historical Society.*

City's propensity to consider nicknames a term of endearment, it likely added to her allure.

One popular form of entertainment that took place beyond the confines of Virginia City's red-light district was known by the French name *tableau vivant*—basically, women posing in various states of undress before a male audience. The *tableau vivant* (French for "living picture") may be thought of as the forerunner of the modern strip club, although in Virginia City, the venues and clientele were generally more sophisticated.

Among the most compelling archival photographs of French women in Virginia City are two that date to the 1870s, when three French actresses arrived with great fanfare. One photograph shows them posed next to an ore car in miners' outfits, complete with boots, hats and lanterns. Doubtless, they had seen many a stage in their American tour, but none had a mine tour thrown in as a little lagniappe.

Marion Goldman noted that, in Victorian times, the word *actress* was a euphemism for a promiscuous woman. To be sure, there were bona fide actresses of national and international fame who did not sell sex on the side, but a large number of lesser-knowns did. According to Goldman (1981), these women "appeared in light dramas and musical evenings, and their ranks included a number of elite prostitutes who traveled from city to city, accepting carefully chosen patrons." Interestingly, she chose one of the photographs of the "Visiting French Actresses" for the cover of her book.

Adah Isaacs Menken

As befitting this talented and successful entertainer, writer and poet, considerable mystery surrounds the early life of Adah Isaacs Menken. Most biographers agree she was born Adelaide McCord in New Orleans in 1835 to mixed-race (black and Creole) parents; she spoke French and Spanish from an early age and was almost certainly raised Catholic (but as an adult, adopted Judaism). She was something of a child prodigy as a dancer and performed at the Opera House in New Orleans and in Havana, Cuba. By the age of nineteen, she moved to Galveston, Texas, and began acting. After a brief first marriage, she and her second husband, Alexander Isaac Menken, launched her career. By 1859 she had appeared on Broadway in a play called *The French Spy*.

The performance that catapulted her to international fame, however, was her interpretation of *Mazeppa*, a play based on a poem by Lord Byron. In this play, she appeared on stage dressed in a flesh-toned body suit and strapped to the back of a horse. It was scandalous, and she was a big hit with the predominantly male Virginia City audience when she became a headliner at Maguire's Opera House in 1864. Writing for *Harper's Magazine*, J. Ross Browne reported on the excitement: "A lady, popularly known as 'The Menken,' had created an immense sensation in San Francisco and was about to favor the citizens of Virginia with a classical equestrian exhibition entitled *Mazeppa*. She was represented as tied in an almost nude state to the back of a wild horse, which was running away with her at a fearful rate of speed." Browne may have been aware of Mark Twain's letter in the *Territorial Enterprise*, dated September 17, 1863, filed from San Francisco. The byline read, "Letter from Mark Twain," and the piece was titled "The Menken—

Written Especially for Gentlemen." It is partially quoted below:

> *When I arrived in San Francisco, I found there was no one in town—at least there was nobody in town but "The Menken."...I went to see her play "Mazeppa," of course. They say she was dressed from head to foot in flesh-colored "tights," but I had no opera glasses, and I couldn't see it, to use the language of the inelegant rabble. She appeared to me to have but one garment on—a thin tight white linen one, of unimportant dimensions.... With the exception of this superfluous rag, the Menken dresses like the Greek slave; but some of her postures are not so modest as the suggestive attitude of the latter. She is a finely formed woman.*

Wells Drury (1936), who did not arrive on the Comstock for another decade, recalled that the 1864 performance was still talked about by those who had witnessed it. "The miners applauded most vociferously for *Mazeppa*," he wrote, and doubtless, "half-dollars were shied onto the stage by the handful." Tossing silver coins onto the stage was, according to Drury, a custom that showed audience appreciation.

The Menken made over $100,000 from her 1863–64 tour of California and Nevada. Although she gained the sobriquet "The Frenzy of Frisco," her adoring fans in Virginia City showed their appreciation in their own unique way. They presented her with a huge silver ingot inscribed, "Miss

Adah Isaacs Menken, circa 1866. *Courtesy of the Library of Congress.*

Adah Isaacs Menken, from friends of Virginia City, Nevada Territory—March 30th 1864." In addition, a mining company christened itself the Menken Shaft and Tunnel Company, and their stock certificates bore a rendering of *Mazeppa*.

Immediately following her successes in the West, Menken took her act to Europe. As a francophone from New Orleans, she naturally gravitated toward Paris. While there, Adah Menken had a scandalous affair with a man twice her age. (She had been married and divorced twice more by then.) He was none other than Alexandre Dumas, the toast of Parisian literati and the author of numerous now-classic works, including *The Three Musketeers* (1844) and *The Count of Monte Cristo* (1844–46). Menken died of an undiagnosed disease at the age of thirty-three on August 10, 1868, and was buried at the Montparnasse Cemetery in Paris.

Nearly a century after her death, the Menken reappeared in America thanks to the popular television show *Bonanza*. The plot of an episode titled "The Magnificent Adah," which aired on November 14, 1959, had Ben, the widower patriarch and owner of the Ponderosa Ranch, rekindle a friendship with Adah, much to the chagrin of his sons, Adam, Hoss and Little Joe. The boys suspected that Adah was a gold digger out to become the next Mrs. Cartwright. The plotting certainly made for high drama, and it was an interesting contrast to an episode that had aired four weeks earlier in which Little Joe fell in love with Virginia City prostitute Julia Bulette.

Julia Bulette

Another mysterious woman with New Orleans connections who left a considerable legacy in Virginia City was Julia Bulette. Although popular during her lifetime, her celebrity—approaching canonization—increased exponentially after her murder in Virginia City on January 20, 1867. She was the darling of the Virginia City Fire Engine Company No. 1, which bestowed on her honorary membership. She became the patron saint of the Virginia City chapter of the Ancient and Honorable Order of *E Clampus Vitus*, a fraternal organization dedicated to Western history, particularly that of nineteenth-century mining towns. Today, to borrow a phrase from Susan James (1984), Julia Bulette is universally acknowledged as the "Queen of Tarts."

According to a recent biography, *The Family Jules: The Life and Times of Julia Bulette* (2011), by C.C. Haile, Bulette was the daughter of a Frenchman

Julia Bulette. *Courtesy of the Nevada Historical Society.*

in New Orleans and an African American mulatta. As such, she was a quadroon, a racial category commonly used in Louisiana to describe someone who was one-quarter black. By the age of sixteen, Julia entered the world's oldest profession in the Crescent City, with her uncle acting as her business manager. She and her uncle eventually moved the "business" to San Francisco to take advantage of the swarm of men drawn there by the California gold rush.

Most biographers, however, claim Julia Bulette was an Englishwoman, born in Liverpool, who later immigrated to New Orleans, married and then divorced her husband and subsequently turned to prostitution in the "Big Easy." Regardless of her nativity, she evidently learned her trade in this country's most celebrated red-light district. Troy Taylor (2010) underscored that "the city was known throughout the country as a cesspool of sin and vice." For a young woman entering the world of sexual commerce in the mid-nineteenth century, New Orleans would have been the graduate school of the profession.

Prostitutes in San Francisco in the late 1850s must have felt the economic slow-down as placer mining along the Mother Lode showed diminishing returns. The era of easy pickings in the goldfields was over. Camp followers, prostitutes among them, constituted a mobile class that followed the money, so it is no wonder that Julia Bulette migrated to Virginia City in 1863. The young boomtown on the east side of the Sierra shone as a beacon.

Contrary to the myth that was developed years after her heinous murder, Julia Bulette was neither beautiful nor rich. Some later biographers even promoted her to the position of a madam and had her dressed in furs and jewels and riding about town in an elegant carriage. In keeping with the Creole queen persona that was created for her, she dined on lavish French cuisine and had her own French maid. In reality, however, Julia Bulette rented a house along D Street in Virginia City's riotous red-light district. The small house lacked both a kitchen and indoor plumbing; it was the antithesis of a palace. Unlike some prostitutes who plied their trade in Virginia City, Bulette evidently never worked in a brothel under the supervision of a madam. As such, she was an independent businesswoman who maintained her own accounts, and at the time of her death, those accounts were in the red. She died in debt, and the money to cover the cost of her funeral came from her benefactors.

One piece of the legend of Julia Bulette that is true and beyond question was her popularity among Virginia City's firefighters, especially Engine Company No. 1 (and not necessarily for obvious reasons). According to the

Territorial Enterprise, she would show up at the occasional conflagration and pitch in by helping to work the fire engine. The only known photograph of Julia Bulette has her posed with a fireman's helmet on the table beside her. The respect she earned from those first responders was evidenced by their leading her funeral procession, decked out in their finest firemen regalia.

No one knows the exact final resting place of Julia Bulette. Time has erased its location, but many years later, some civic boosters erected a headstone surrounded with a white picket fence in the old Flowery Hill Cemetery. It became an instant tourist attraction for those who revel in lore and legend. Speaking of her legacy, Susan James (1984) wrote, "The legend of Julia Bulette may be filled with inaccuracies, but it is a good story whose embroideries make it one of the most captivating examples of Comstock folklore."

Envoi

When a member of Virginia City's French community was shot and killed on March 31, 1892, while attempting to protect his sister's husband, the city praised his bravery and mourned his loss. Alf Doten noted the details in his journal.

> *About 8 o'clock last evening, August Bouheben, brother-in-law of A. Laigneau, the coffee dealer on South C Street, was fatally shot by Jerry Barry, a miner in the Yellow Jacket Mine. It was at Laigneau's store in a dispute or discussion about money matters, between Barry and Laigneau. Barry drew a pistol and Bouheben, in trying to prevent his shooting Laigneau by wrestling with him for the pistol, got shot in the head, from which he died this PM.*

The French contributed mightily to the ethnic quilt that was Virginia City. Their love of life—wine, women and song—and general disregard for the rigid strictures of Victorian America were character traits that were much admired.

7

STOCK SWINDLES

In January, stocks took a big rise, and Chollar went to $89. I sold. She went on up to $99, and I bought it back, losing $10, as my friends said. But two days later, she went up to $320. I then sold it again. I had now made a handsome profit of $231 per share. I had also bought some Sierra Nevada for $24 the same week and sold it for $44 in three days' time.
—Mary McNair Matthews

The stock-trading frenzy associated with the boom period of the Comstock Lode is legendary, as illustrated by *Territorial Enterprise* writers Dan De Quille and Mark Twain. Dan De Quille (1876) devoted considerable ink to the trading of mining stock in Virginia City. He wrote, "During the prevalence of a big stock excitement...Virginia City hums like a Brobdingnagian beehive." In *Roughing It* (1872), Mark Twain described how "a wild spirit possessed the mining brain of the community." Even Mary McNair Matthews (1880) confessed that she got stock fever and "had a handsome fortune invested in stocks."

The San Francisco Stock Exchange was established in 1862 as a direct response to the incredible quantities of gold and silver coming out of the Comstock. In the three years after the discovery of the lode, mining companies had largely replaced individual prospectors and small groups of miners working cooperatively. The capital requirements of underground mining could no longer be met by simple grubstake. Then as now, publicly traded companies raised money through the sale of stock, which allowed them to grow and show a profit.

To be sure, there existed honest, hardworking folks on the Comstock, in San Francisco and elsewhere who invested their cash in mining stocks with a reasonable expectation of profit; among them was the aforementioned Mary McNair Matthews. Others, however, viewed the wild world of the San Francisco Stock Exchange as an environment ripe for massive swindle. This latter group included, incredibly, some mining companies themselves.

In addition to investors profiting from a rise in the value of their stock, there was the assumption that a dividend would be paid on occasion. More often, however, mining companies went back to stockholders for an assessment, a method of raising additional capital on existing shares of stock. Five years into the San Francisco Stock Exchange, Comstock mining companies numbered roughly four hundred, only a few of which paid dividends. The most egregious example of swindling where assessments were concerned was the Bullion Mine; described as a "spectacular fraud," its actual production of precious metal amounted to zero, yet it managed to levy assessments from shareholders in the amount of $3.8 million.

THE SILVER MANIA AT SAN FRANCISCO.

J. Ross Browne illustration, "The Silver Mania at San Francisco." *Author's collection.*

One of the most notorious tactics to manipulate stock prices was the sequestering of miners. Mine supervisors, doubtless at the request of their superiors, occasionally prevented miners from ascending their underground workings at the conclusion of their shifts. They also kept the next shift from descending. This obvious interruption in the work routine had the desired effect; word spread quickly, with the assumption that a rich vein of precious metal had been discovered and that the mine owners wanted to keep it under wraps. Naturally, the stock price would soar, and those in the know would cash in just before the hoax was revealed.

Without a doubt, the worst swindle of those wanting to cash in on the Comstock boom came in the form of completely bogus mining stock. The sale of fraudulent stock generally did not work within the precincts of the Comstock itself or its immediate hinterland. Instead, anyone with a printing press and a bit of artistic flair could "issue" stock whose buyers resided hundreds or thousands of miles away. These investors often lived on the East Coast or in Europe and were easily duped.

Scams were not limited to mining stock; one outrageous example was the promotion of the Reese River Navigation Company and the sale of bogus stock. Simply put, north-central Nevada's Reese River is hardly a river, and it most certainly is not navigable, except perhaps by canoe for a few weeks in the spring following a particularly wet winter.

Most people who traded in mining stock were aware of the risks, but as J. Ross Browne, writing for *Harper's Magazine*, observed in 1863, "Silver mania had taken possession of the entire population [of San Francisco], without distinction of age or sex." According to early stock certificates, shareholders possessed a specific portion of the mine as measured in feet. Browne described the scene.

> *Every office was an emporium for the purchase and sale of feet; every desk in every store was a stall at which millionaires browsed upon paper; every window glared and dazzled the sight with gorgeous engravings of stocks; every man of the hundreds and tens of hundreds that stood at every corner, and in every saloon, and before every bar, carried feet in his pockets and dividends in his eyes; and every walking thing, save horses and dogs and rats and mice, talked stocks and feet from morning 'till night, and dreamed dividends from night 'till morning.*

The same could be said of Virginia City, where even an otherwise conservative widow from back East could not resist the lure of a get-rich-quick investment.

Being a reporter for the *Territorial Enterprise* had its perquisites, and one, according to Mark Twain in *Roughing It* (1872), was the receipt of feet in mining stock in exchange for newspaper publicity for the claim. "New claims were taken up daily, and it was the friendly custom to run straight to the newspaper offices, give the reporters forty or fifty 'feet,' and get them to go and examine the mine and publish a notice of it." Twain explained that he and other reporters never failed to accept the "feet," and their "praise" could easily be deciphered by discerning readers.

Virginia City had some especially discerning readers, among them was John Mackay. Mackay arrived on the Comstock shortly after the 1859 discovery, worked as a four-dollar-per-day miner, became intimately acquainted with the seemingly inscrutable ore body and ultimately parlayed his ability to read the geology of the lode into a personal fortune. He, along with his partners, James Fair, James Flood and William O'Brien—known collectively as the "Bonanza Kings"—became some of the wealthiest men in America. Although John Mackay and his partners understood the pitfalls of the stock market, whenever he was asked for a stock tip, he invariably replied that the safest place for someone's money was in the bank.

SPECULATORS V. INVESTORS

In a retrospective of the boom period, Lord (1883) argued that a distinction should be made between speculators and investors, the former being little distinguished from gamblers. He wrote, "To stock speculators, accurate valuations are generally objectionable, as they tend to prevent stock deals, which are their harvest. Now, it was unfortunately true that, since the San Francisco Stock Exchange became one of the most flourishing institutions of that city, men began to buy mining stocks, as a rule, for speculative purposes and not as an investment." There were occasional demands for greater "transparency," to borrow a term now wistfully applied to political decision-making. The *Territorial Enterprise* advocated for the submission of detailed quarterly reports as a method of "dissipating the fog which hung over the management of the Comstock Mines."

Unfortunately, stock speculation and corporate fog remained endemic to American commerce for another fifty years after the end of the Comstock's

Big Bonanza. Grant Smith, in *The History of the Comstock Lode* (1943), wrote, "Those of us who lived through that hectic Comstock period and, as well, through more recent mad speculative eras which have left millions in this country ruined and hopeless, are unable to see any difference between the two periods."

CAVEAT EMPTOR?

Although there were indications some weeks beforehand, everyone knew by "Black Tuesday," October 29, 1929, that the American economy and way of life was in crisis. The stock market crash was a historic punctuation; what preceded it was a decade of prosperity (the Roaring Twenties) and what succeeded it was the opposite (the Great Depression). Like all economic fluctuations, there was no simple cause and effect, but excessive stock speculation has since been singled out as an important catalyst. President Herbert Hoover and his financial advisors believed the economy would recover without federal intervention. Hoover's successor, Franklin D. Roosevelt, thought differently. In addition to the popular and successful make-work programs, Roosevelt instituted significant infrastructural improvements and financial reforms, including the creation of the U.S. Securities and Exchange Commission (SEC) in 1934.

The mission statement of the SEC identifies investor protection as its primary *raison d'*être. Since 1934, publicly traded companies have been required to file financial statements, reports to stockholders and other pertinent documents with the SEC. These are available to the public in the belief that knowledge constitutes the best protection for the investor. It is interesting that Eliot Lord held the same opinion in 1883. It is also ironic that Mark Twain, who witnessed fortunes made and lost while reporting for the *Territorial Enterprise*, himself made bad investments totaling nearly $200,000 and declared bankruptcy in 1894.

There existed a curious relationship between the Comstock and presidential politics. On October 29, 1879, former president Ulysses S. Grant visited Virginia City. Bonanza kings John Mackay and James Fair gave him a personal underground mine tour. President Grant was impressed, and he thought the boom would last for years to come—it would not. Five decades to the day later, President Herbert Hoover was unimpressed by Black Tuesday and thought the stock market would soon correct itself—it did not.

"What Show Have You Got, Little Man?" *Puck* magazine, April 8, 1908. *Illustration by Udo J. Keppler. Courtesy of the Library of Congress.*

Herbert Clark Hoover, the thirty-first president of the United States, was among the first class to graduate from Stanford University in 1895. There, he studied to become a mining engineer and doubtless read Eliot Lord's (1883) now-classic work on the Comstock. In addition, he had hands-on experience in the mining industry; his first job after graduation was in a Nevada County, California, gold mine, and he later ventured up to the Klondike, where he met Jack London. It is tempting to speculate about how his familiarity with the Comstock Lode and his mining background may have tempered his views on the stock market in 1929. Did his knowledge of Western mining—its booms and busts—contribute to his laissez-faire attitude on the stock market?

The epigram "the more things change, the more they remain the same" certainly applies to the stock market. From the wild ride of the San Francisco Stock Market in the 1860s and 1870s to the present day, investment remains synonymous with risks and rewards. Although the SEC provides some degree of regulation and federal oversight today, the stock market still has its seamy side, where manipulators, insider traders and out-and-out swindlers manage to make money at the expense of investors. However, it also is a place where individuals like Mary McNair Matthews can invest their money and realize their dreams. What happens on Wall Street every trading day today would be recognizable to Virginia City residents who flocked to the broadsheets posted on C Street.

8
CROOKED LAWYERS AND POLITICIANS

The first exploiters of the lode left behind a record of confusion, waste, and chicanery rather worse than that of most frontier mining camps. A web of boundary disputes clogged the courts and periodically brought operations to a standstill; the judiciary was weak and venal (a judge was considered reprehensibly lax only if he sold out to both sides), elections were decided by open bribery, and desperadoes from all over the West swaggered, unmolested, through the streets and bars, robbing and cheating and killing with impunity.
—Oscar Lewis

Everyone is familiar with lawyer jokes. The basis of their humor is a set of derogatory traits deemed universal to the profession. For example, "Question: How does an attorney sleep? Answer: First, he lies on one side, then he lies on the other." People have derided lawyers since the time of William Shakespeare—if not before—and members of the legal profession on the Comstock were not exempt from public ridicule. In fact, the practice of law in Storey County, Nevada, during the boom years provided us with some of the most egregious examples of legal chicanery, as well as some of funniest satire.

Politicians, many of whom began their careers as lawyers, had a reputation among the general public for feeding at the public trough. Their behavior frequently exhibited a single-minded focus on self-aggrandizement rather than concern for the public good, which led to a stereotype that persists to this day. Many Nevadans who held offices in Carson City or Washington,

D.C., in the late nineteenth century could trace their rise to political power directly back to having made their bundle in Virginia City. They, too, were the butts of jokes. One of the jokes that is most often quoted came from Mark Twain: "Suppose you were an idiot. Now, suppose you were a member of Congress. But I repeat myself."

LAWYERS

Virginia City contained a large percentage of lawyers per capita due to the money being made in the area. With conflicting mining claims and fortunes at stake, the place was a cash cow for lawyers representing both plaintiffs and defendants. According to Drury (1936), "It was the most prolific place for litigation and lawyers on earth, for every inch was covered with claims three or four deep." Regardless of the outcome of their cases, they earned their fees, which were enormous. This irked some who needed legal services for less remunerative cases, such as Mary McNair Matthews (1880), who remarked, "It is a shame the way lawyers act—will never take a case for a poor person."

It is ironic that attorneys shied away from the legal causes of people of modest means, like the widow Matthews, because many of them came from similarly modest, if not impoverished, circumstances. Training in the law often meant going through a period of apprenticeship with an established lawyer who possessed a small legal library. It did not even require the equivalent of a high school education—let alone a college degree. Although there were actual law schools at the time, such as Harvard Law School (established in 1817), many lawyers on the Western mining frontier resembled self-taught Abraham Lincoln.

Unquestionably, the most successful lawyer on the Comstock was William Morris Stewart. Stewart grew up in upstate New York, briefly attended Yale and, in 1850, joined the horde who rushed to the California Mother Lode. His efforts in the goldfields of the Sierra Foothills were disappointing, so he apprenticed in the field of law and actually served as the acting attorney general of California before moving to Nevada in 1860.

William Stewart arrived on the Comstock at an important transitional period in mining. Hundreds of small claims and workings were being consolidated by corporate interests, resulting in a courtroom battle over the nature of underground gold and silver deposits. Independent miners and

J. Ross Browne illustration, "The Smooths." *Author's collection.*

the smaller companies advocated for a "many ledge" theory, holding that multiple separate ledges existed in close proximity. This was a theory that would justify their claims and perpetuate their access to their small lodes. In opposition, newly formed mining companies with deep pockets subscribed to a "single ledge" theory, the idea that the mineralization beneath Mount Davidson actually derived from one great geologic fault.

The confusion that existed above ground among competing mining claimants was nothing compared to what was happening underground. Miners in the Ophir and an adjacent mine, the Burning Moscow, found themselves following veins of ore that were being worked by their neighbors. When fisticuffs failed to resolve the issue, it was brought before territorial judge Gordon N. Mott. The case languished, Mott retired and the owners of the Ophir, who favored a "single ledge" theory, resumed their intrusion into the Burning Moscow.

Judge Mott's replacement for the Nevada Territorial Judiciary was John Wesley North, who made it known he supported the "many ledge" theory. This opinion reverberated underground when the Burning Moscow

J. Ross Browne illustration, "A Question of Title." *Author's collection.*

superintendent, armed with a warrant and two deputy sheriffs, cleared out the Ophir interlopers. Then entered attorney William Stewart. In his book *The Bonanza King: John Mackay and the Battle Over the Greatest Riches in the American West* (2018), Gregory Crouch described the contest as follows:

> *Many-ledge advocates considered the one-ledgers evil corporate monopolists; the one-ledge companies thought the many-ledgers were thieves. The weight of underground evidence mounting in favor of the Comstock Lode's being one single, gigantic fissure vein did little to contain public ire against the legal skullduggery they propagated to strengthen their holdings. Shrewd, forceful, politically manipulative mining attorney William M. Stewart cleaned up a fortune representing the leading mines and the one-ledge theory.*

Stewart, following the money in a time-honored lawyerly fashion, had permanently aligned himself with the wealthy elite. Ronald James (1998) summarized the significance of this legal win. "His San Francisco employers won their case in court and maintained their dominant interest in the Comstock. With the ore body perceived as a single ledge, it would be difficult, if not impossible, for a lucky prospector to strike it rich with a new claim on the Comstock." For his efforts on their behalf, William Stewart made an estimated $500,000, a tidy sum even by today's standards. William Stewart played a significant role in achieving statehood for Nevada and subsequently went on to serve as a U.S. Senator from Nevada for nearly thirty years. He is probably the Silver State's quintessential lawyer-turned-politician.

Adjudication of mining disputes dominated the courtroom during the Comstock Lode's first six years and cost the litigants an estimated $10 million, or roughly one-fifth of the value of ore extracted during that period. Afterward, the place settled into legal squabbles typical of other communities, although they often had a flair that was unique to Virginia City.

Some attorneys specialized in divorce, which was a common occurrence at the height of the Comstock Lode. According to Mary McNair Matthews (1880), "There is hardly a week but there is an application for a divorce. Virginia City is truly a city of divorces." She went on to explain the unusually high divorce rate. "A good match with them [women on the Comstock] means a man with money. Now, this is a very foolish thing, for they may marry a millionaire today, and in six months, they will be the wife of a poor man. Ask them how it happened, and their answer will be, dealing in stocks or gambling—as often one as the other."

Senator William Stewart. *Courtesy of the Library of Congress.*

Some of the most sensational legal cases of the day involved suits against men who made fortunes on the Comstock. The most common involved either disgruntled stockholders or affairs of the heart. One of the most laughable of the latter category was a lawsuit claiming that millionaire John Mackay had an affair with the wife of a man by the name of William Smallman. The husband-and-wife plaintiffs alleged Mackay had "unlawful intimacy" with Mrs. Smallman in 1878 and sought a judgment of $200,000. Unfortunately, their attorney had not done his homework because Mackay and his wife were on a European tour at the time the supposed affair took place. The case was dismissed.

Other cases, however, were not so easily dismissed. Whereas John Mackay, by all accounts, was an honorable and devoted family man, his business partner, James Fair, was just the opposite. Fair had the reputation of being a notorious philanderer—in Virginia City, in San Francisco and in Washington, D.C., while serving as a U.S. senator for Nevada. Theresa, his long-suffering wife, finally filed for divorce in San Francisco on May 12, 1883, on the grounds of "habitual adultery." In this case, the attorney representing the plaintiff's wife presented overwhelming evidence, including the testimony of two San Francisco prostitutes, and won a judgment of $4.25 million.

Although the City by the Bay saw some high-profile legal battles, such as Fair's divorce and a posthumous case involving the estate of William Sharon, the Storey County Courthouse in Virginia City had its share of judicial drama. In fact, the courthouse itself—or rather, its prominent statue of Lady Justice—may symbolize the community's take on the law. Lady Justice, with her scales and sword, normally appears blindfolded, which is meant to represent impartiality in the eyes of the law. The statue that adorns the façade of Virginia City's impressive Italianate courthouse (built in 1876) is not blindfolded.

There have been various interpretations of what a fully sighted Lady Justice meant to Virginia City residents during the Big Bonanza. Could she

Lady Justice statue, Storey County Courthouse. *Courtesy of Robin Johnson.*

Storey County Courthouse. *Courtesy of Robin Johnson.*

represent the opposite of impartiality in the eyes of the law, a frontier justice epitomized by Judge Roy Bean, who meted out harsh convictions from the bench in Val Verde County, Texas? This is disputed by former Nevada State Historic Preservation Officer Ronald James, who wrote in *Temples of Justice: County Courthouses of Nevada* (1994), "The fact that she lacks a blindfold was probably not, as is maintained by local lore, a commentary on frontier justice." All symbolism aside, Virginia City's Lady Justice witnessed some incredible courtroom proceedings.

Lady Justice was undoubtedly aware of all the money changing hands inside the Storey County Courthouse. It was no secret that jurors could be bought, as could witnesses. Members of the bar knew their cases were won or lost based on which side distributed the most liberal bribes. Even judges were not immune to selling their opinions to the highest bidder.

The courthouse was also a source of entertainment for the community. An earlier court building, which burned in the great conflagration of 1875, gained a reputation for its crowd-pleasing hijinks. One of the funniest involved the composition of a jury. One sheriff fulfilled his obligation of assembling a jury in a most amusing way by routinely selecting twelve men from among the Virginia City citizenry with similar characteristics—tall men, short men, thin or fat men—even ugly men. People would stop by the courthouse just to see the jury and get a good laugh.

Some cases that came before the court ended in unexpected rulings, but in retrospect, the judgment made perfect sense when seen from the unique perspective of life on the Comstock. Wells Drury (1936) related one such case:

> *A roisterer sued in Virginia City for defective sidewalks, which had caused a grievous bodily injury to him on a spree. The defendants objected that the man was drunk. The judge ruled in favor of the plaintiff, handing down the sage opinion that a drunken man is entitled to good sidewalks as much as a sober man and needs them a great deal more.*

POLITICIANS

One of the best books about politicians in the post–Civil War era is *The Gilded Age: A Tale of Today* (1873) by Mark Twain and Charles Dudley Warner. Although it is a work of fiction, it portrays life in and around America's halls of power in a most believable way. Sam Clemens and his Hartford, Connecticut neighbor Charles Warner did not make up the story out of whole cloth. Its biting satire of Washington politics and the rich and powerful had a considerable basis in fact, some of which had a very real Virginia City connection.

Two years prior to the publication of *The Innocents Abroad* (1869), the book that made Mark Twain a household name, he spent a brief period in our nation's capital working as a congressional aide to Senator William M. Stewart, the same William Stewart who rose to prominence by winning the "single ledge" v. "many ledge" case on the Comstock. Sam Clemens also worked for Nevada's other senator, James Nye, who had formerly served as governor of the Nevada Territory while Sam's brother Orion was the territorial secretary. He obviously knew Stewart and Nye in Virginia City and Carson City, and he parlayed those relationships into a job that would temporarily subsidize his writing career.

Unlike today, members of Congress did not have a staff per se. They often hired newspaper reporters who willing to moonlight, and thus, Senator Stewart, who knew Mark Twain when he worked for the *Territorial Enterprise*, hired him. Stewart even found Clemens a room in the same Washington boardinghouse where he himself was staying. Their work together did not last long, and Stewart commented in his memoir, *Reminiscences of Senator William M. Stewart, of Nevada* (1908), "I was confident that [Twain] would come to no good end, but…I understand he has settled down and become respectable."

Sam Clemens actually knew a thing or two about the workings of a legislative body. He covered the Nevada territorial legislature as a cub reporter, which is where he found his irreverent voice. Consider this description of the floor of the legislature: "covered…with clean sawdust by way of carpet and spittoon combined." Twain used his experience in Washington as fodder for *The Gilded Age*. While reading his satire of the maelstrom that was Washington power, politics and money, one is often amazed by how little things have changed. The following is Twain poking fun at government spending: "That building is the Capitol; gossips will tell you that by the original estimates, it was to cost $12,000,000, and that the government did come within $21,200,000 of building it for that sum."

There was actually a lot to horrify voters who naively believed elected officials were public servants, but Nevadans familiar with the mighty men of Virginia City knew better. They knew seats in the United States Senate—"the World's Most Exclusive Club"—were bought. Before the passage of the Seventeenth Amendment to the U.S. Constitution in 1913, senators, unlike representatives to Congress, were not elected by popular vote. Instead, they were selected by state legislatures. Buying votes, therefore, was simplified. Candidates targeted members of the legislature and distributed funds sufficient to ensure a majority.

Among the earliest U.S. senators from Nevada, four began their careers on the Comstock—William M. Stewart, John P. Jones, William Sharon and James G. Fair—and collectively, they spent millions. In his 1874 campaign, William Sharon strategically distributed Ophir shares to Nevada legislators. He also bought the opposition newspaper, Virginia City's *Territorial Enterprise*,

"Senatorial Courtesy." William Stewart addressing the U.S. Senate. *Puck* magazine, October 18, 1893. *Illustration by Louis Dalrymple. Courtesy of the Library of Congress.*

William Sharon. *Courtesy of the Special Collections Department, University of Nevada–Reno Libraries.*

for five times its value. (So much for freedom of the press.) At a time when ad hominem and libelous remarks were an expected part of political rhetoric, Sharon's opposition, with a comparatively smaller war chest, called him "the scrawny little Midas."

William Sharon's six-year term as U.S. senator from Nevada was a farce. He preferred living in San Francisco and rarely made an appearance in the state he represented or the city on the Potomac where he was supposed to be doing the people's business. Senate roll calls indicate he was present for less than 1 percent of his tenure. Although Sharon was said to relish the title "senator," he clearly put his own business interests, such as the Bank of California, first and foremost. In *The Infamous King of the Comstock: William Sharon and the Gilded Age in the West* (2006), Michael Makley referred to this chapter of Senator Sharon's career as "an ill-fitting toga." All that money spent for an unused political office is beyond understanding, unless, of course, you think of it as just another status acquisition of a wealthy man.

The other Nevada senators with Comstock roots were more productive than Sharon. How could they not be? William Stewart, who served for nearly thirty years in the U.S. Senate (1865–75 and 1887–1905), actually accomplished quite a bit, including his signature piece of legislation, the General Mining Act of 1872. Its purpose was to allow mining on public lands, as well as facilitate settlement in the West. Despite criticism that the law basically handed over publicly owned valuable minerals to private corporations—even foreign corporations—it remains enforced to this day.

John P. Jones was born in England in 1829, grew up in Ohio and, at the age of twenty, joined the rush west to the California goldfields. He moved to Gold Hill, Nevada, in 1868 and made a name for himself on the Comstock as the superintendent of the Crown Point Mine. He and his business partner, Alvinza Hayward, made a fortune from the Crown Point, which allowed Jones to "purchase" a senate seat that he kept for thirty years (1873–1903). Although he had a reputation for being an entertaining storyteller on the Senate floor, his views on immigration were incredibly racist. An immigrant himself, he favored legislation that limited or excluded those who were not from northern and western Europe—most especially the Chinese.

Like Senator Jones, James G. Fair also participated in the California gold rush before migrating to the Comstock. He worked as superintendent of the Ophir Mine before he famously partnered with Mackay, Flood and O'Brien, becoming part of the Bonanza kings' foursome. He served as U.S. senator from Nevada for a six-year term (1881–87) following the Comstock's peak mining period. Fair, too, was an immigrant (from Northern Ireland), and he shared Senator Jones's views on immigration. His ardent support for the Chinese Exclusion Act of 1882 received praise from many Nevada constituents, but that was negated by his scandalous personal life.

It may seem counterintuitive that the richest man on the Comstock, John W. Mackay, had no interest in seeking public office. In Michael Makley's (2009) biography of John Mackay, he quoted Mackay as saying, "I have no taste for political life, and nothing could induce me to enter it." Perhaps this reluctance to seek public office stemmed from his humble, unassuming and common-man persona—or maybe he was just too darn honest.

EPILOGUE

The fortunes of the Comstock mining district are now [in 1881] *depressed.*
—*Eliot Lord*

Beginning as early as the 1930s, a strange transformation occurred on the Comstock. What had been a dormant, even dying, mining district slowly blossomed into a magnet for artists, literati, and others who wished to experience something of the fast-disappearing Wild West.
—*Ronald M. James*

Mining boomtowns, by definition, inevitably experienced a bust. The trajectory from *bonanza* to *borrasca* played out from town to town all over the West, and Virginia City was no exception. Why this happened is no mystery; precious metal deposits were a finite resource and could not be mined forever. What James "Old Virginny" Finney, Henry "Pancake" Comstock and a cadre of ragtag prospectors started in 1859 had reached near exhaustion two decades later. Virginia City's last hurrah was a visit from former president Ulysses S. Grant in late October 1879. Bonanza kings John Mackay and James Fair personally escorted Grant and his family on an excursion into the Stygian depths of the Comstock Lode. On his return to sunshine and crisp, fresh air, the president quipped, "That's as close to hell as I ever want to get!" What Grant saw, however, was the end of an era.

Ulysses S. Grant and party after a Virginia City mine tour, 1879. *Photograph by Noe & Lee. Courtesy of the Special Collections Department, University of Nevada–Reno Libraries.*

The Big Bonanza was the beating heart of the Comstock. After the ore pinched out in the deep mines, the prognosis was terminal. Mine owners and shareholders knew additional work would be costly and futile. As if pulling the plug on life support, the giant pumps of the Con Virginia and California Mines, which supplied air and drained water, stopped for good on October 16, 1886. Other shallower mines continued operations for another dozen years or so, but the downward economic trend resembled the steep slope of Mount Davidson.

The reduction in rich ore, which had become obvious to all, created lasting repercussions. Virginia City's best brothel, the Brick, was sold in 1892. The U.S. Mint in Carson City produced its last run of gold and silver coins in 1893. Mining companies paid their final dividends in 1895. In 1897, Virginia City's St. Mary Louise Hospital closed, as did the best saloon in town, the Washoe Club. These business closures corresponded to a slow but steady exodus of the area's population. As James (1998) noted, "Low-grade ore in the upper levels provided marginal subsistence for the industrial complex." The gleaners of gold and silver persisted. By the turn of the century, however, yield from the Comstock mines fell below the cost of production, and the U.S. decennial census for 1900 reflected this eclipse—only 3,560 residents, one-fifth of the Big Bonanza population, remained in the whole of Storey County.

EPILOGUE

As the mines of the legendary Comstock Lode lost their profitability, a heretofore unknown bonanza revealed itself in central Nevada. The towns of Tonopah and Goldfield boomed in the first decade of the twentieth century; the latter, with a population of thirty thousand, became Nevada's largest city. This rush to northern Nye County siphoned off people, businesses, mining equipment and even entire buildings from Virginia City.

The mining industry did not entirely abandon the Comstock, however. A new method of open pit (as opposed to underground) mining was tried in the early 1930s. A handful of companies acquired the rights to the principal claims on the Comstock, and one of them, the Arizona Comstock Company, began gouging out a massive pit on the west side of South C Street. The Loring Cut, named for Arizona Comstock director William J. Loring, did not make money for its investors. Mining ceased at the Loring Cut, but the scar remains part of Virginia City's historical landscape.

Like the phoenix rising from the ashes, Virginia City emerged from the Great Depression and World War II, thanks to several fortuitous circumstances. The "divorce trade" blossomed after Nevada shortened its residency requirement in 1931 to a mere six weeks. Many celebrities who sought divorces temporarily moved to Reno and, when looking for ways to while away the time, discovered the historical ambiance of Virginia City. That same year, Nevada reinstated legalized gambling, which had been on hiatus for twenty-two years. Finally, the 1933 passage of the Twenty-First Amendment, which repealed Prohibition, brought the saloon trade back to life. It was a perfect storm for Virginia City.

The old boomtown, which was then in a state of decay, became a favorite haunt for people who were drawn to its Old West heritage and lingering lifestyle. One group of notables—Lucius Beebe, Katherine Best, Walter Van Tilburg Clark, Charles Clegg, Duncan Emrich and Katherine Hillyer—actually made Virginia City their home. Emrich was the first to put down roots. When not working in Washington, D.C., as the director of the folklore section of the Library of Congress, he was in Virginia City. Beebe and Clegg soon followed. They bought John Piper's house on A Street and revived the *Territorial Enterprise*. Best and Hillyer, freelance writers who were known as "the Katies," bought a two-story house on D Street across from the Mackay Mansion. Clark, the most well-known and the last to leave in an animated sense, bought a house on Stewart Street. He died in 1971 and was buried in Virginia City's Silver Terrace Cemetery.

In her chapter in *Comstock Women* (1998) titled "Girls of the Golden West," Andria Taylor wrote, "While the 1940s Comstock writers were sophisticates,

Bucket of Blood Saloon, 1935. *Photograph by Gus Bundy. Courtesy of the Special Collections Department, University of Nevada–Reno Libraries.*

they were fascinated by lowlife figures—the drunks and the prostitutes." These intellectuals loved wicked Virginia City, in all its sordid decay. They also worked to breathe new life into the place, especially the flamboyant Lucius Beebe and Charles Clegg. Writing in the magazine *Nevada in the West* (2011), Michael "Bert" Bedeau explained how Beebe and Clegg promoted the town through architectural restoration and journalism:

> *Rehabilitation of what came to be known as the Piper-Beebe House was one of the first historic preservation efforts in Virginia City—marking a significant effort in the struggle to save the Comstock's fast disappearing architectural heritage. House renovation was followed by the purchase of the long defunct Territorial Enterprise newspaper....By 1954, with Beebe and Clegg and many literary friends contributing, the Enterprise achieved the widest circulation of any weekly on the West Coast. It quickly became something of a national cultural phenomenon.*

Piper-Beebe House, A Street. *Courtesy of Robin Johnson.*

Walter Van Tilburg Clark was the only local writer, more or less. His father served as the president of the University of Nevada in Reno, which is where the younger Clark received his undergraduate and graduate education. Clark became a university professor and fiction writer. Two of his novels, *The Ox-Bow Incident* (1940) and *Track of the Cat* (1949), became films, starring Henry Fonda and Robert Mitchum, respectively. His novel *The City of Trembling Leaves* (1945), which is set in Reno, is a wonderful coming-of-age story that is a thinly veiled autobiography. Clark and his wife loved living in Virginia City, and his lasting contribution to the Comstock came when he devoted the last decade of his life to transcribing and editing the journals of Alf Doten.

Virginia City gained national notoriety in 1959, when the hit television series *Bonanza* was first aired. The fictious Ponderosa Ranch encompassed a huge area between Lake Tahoe and Virginia City, and many of the 431 episodes featured the Cartwrights—played by Lorne Greene, Dan Blocker, Michael Landon and Pernell Roberts—in Virginia City, or more

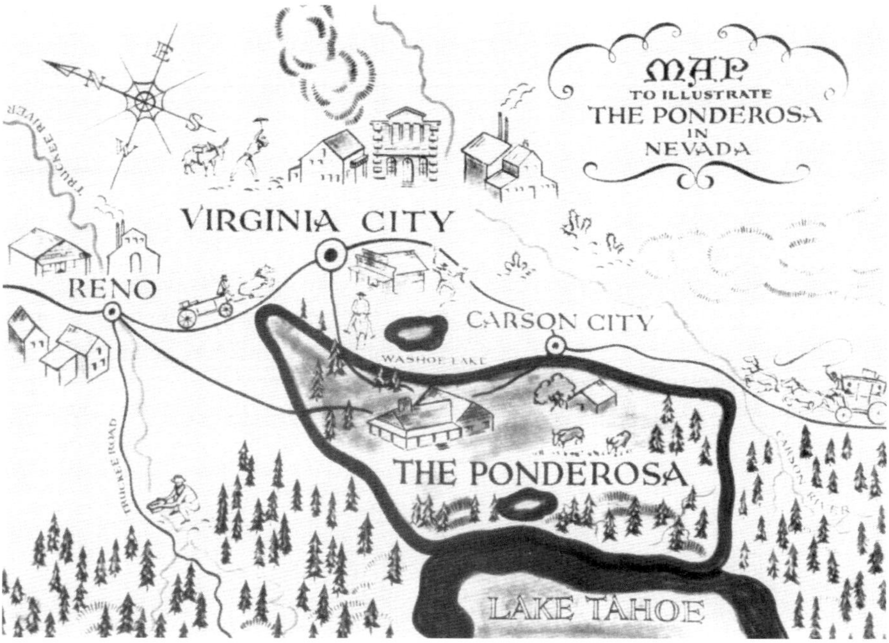

Map of the Ponderosa Ranch for the television show *Bonanza*. *Artwork by Robert Temple Ayers. Courtesy of the Nevada State Library and Archives.*

correctly, a set meant to resemble Virginia City. The writers of *Bonanza* took considerable license when presenting the place and its history. Ronald James (1998) pointed out, "It mattered little that their Virginia City stood on level ground…[and was] a place that chiefly served ranchers who drove their wagons into town for supplies, a drink in a local saloon, and invariably a little trouble." America loved it, regardless of these inaccuracies.

One consequence of *Bonanza*, which made a weekly appearance in American households from the Comstock centennial in 1959 until 1973, was that it stimulated tourism. People wanted to see Virginia City—and not necessarily the Virginia City of the literati. The public expected the Cartwright's Virginia City, and the town delivered; building façades became more rustic, costumed gunslingers strolled the boarded sidewalks and souvenir shops did a land office business. Some locals and more than a few historians referred to this makeover as the "Bonanzafication" of Virginia City.

Another chapter in the evolution of Virginia City came from an unexpected source. Several years before Scott McKenzie sang, "If you're going to San

Francisco, be sure to wear some flowers in your hair," and young people converged on the corner of Haight and Ashbury Streets in what became known as the "Summer of Love" (1967), hippies discovered the Comstock. They dressed in Western garb, carried guns, smoked pot, dropped acid and played rock and roll. The Red Dog Saloon on North C Street became the epicenter of a movement, with San Francisco bands like Big Brother and the Holding Company and the Charlatans making regular appearances.

Most people who reflect on the counterculture movement of the 1960s trace its roots back to the City by the Bay, but in the documentary *The Life and Times of the Red Dog Saloon* (1996), filmmaker Mary Works pointed out the seminal role of Virginia City. "If the psychedelic sixties were born in the dancehalls of San Francisco, then they were conceived in a saloon in a small Western mining town, where the musicians carried Winchesters, the kitchen served French gourmet meals, and the cocktail waitress packed a doorknob for subduing rowdy customers." The Red Dog, which is now under new ownership, still maintains a countercultural vibe; it still pours drinks and hosts musicians, and its walls are plastered with posters from the 1960s.

Virginia City continues to reinvent itself, but tourism is central. Two million visitors flock to the Comstock every year. Quirky events, such as camel races and outhouse races, have been crowd pleasers for decades.

Virginia City from the cemetery, 1940. *Courtesy of the Library of Congress.*

Parades, chili cook-offs and motorcycle gatherings all have their appeal, and they bring in people and dollars. But at this old mining town's core is its lore, legend and persistent way of life.

James "Old Virginny" Finney's namesake was a hard place—a double entendre used by geographer Richard Francaviglia to describe historic mining landscapes and livelihoods—but it was a hard place fondly remembered by many who lived it. Former publisher of the *Territorial Enterprise* Joe Goodman was one such person. Long after he left the Comstock for greener pastures, he waxed poetic:

> *The site was bleak, the houses small,*
> *The narrow streets unpaved and slanting,*
> *But now it seems to me of all*
> *The spots on earth the most enchanting.*

Virginia City remains the personification of a gritty mining town with a veneer of Victorian charm. It is a tourist town now, but that is not necessarily a pejorative. Residents and visitors alike appreciate and celebrate what took place in the town, the fortunes that were made and lost there and its devil-may-care attitude. For many, life in Virginia City during its nineteenth-century heyday may be summed up in one word: wicked.

BIBLIOGRAPHY

This bibliography of sources is not comprehensive, insofar as the literature on Virginia City is vast, but the books and articles listed below are what the author found most useful in his research. They are largely nonfictional, but some works of fiction are included because they give the reader a wonderful sense of place.

Angel, Myron, ed. *History of Nevada*. Oakland, CA: Thompson and West, 1881.

Barnhart, Jacqueline Baker. *The Fair But Frail: Prostitution in San Francisco, 1849–1900*. Reno: University of Nevada Press, 1986.

Bedeau, Michael A. "Bert." "Beebe & Clegg on the Comstock." *Nevada in the West* magazine, Spring 2011.

Beebe, Lucius. *Comstock Commotion: The Story of the Territorial Enterprise*. Palo Alto, CA: Stanford University Press, 1954.

Beebe, Lucius, and Charles Clegg. *Legends of the Comstock Lode*. Oakland, CA: Grahame H. Hardy, 1950.

Berkove, Lawrence I., ed. *Dan De Quille Dives and Lazarus: Their Wanderings and Adventures in the Infernal Regions*. Ann Arbor, MI: Ardis Publishers, 1988.

Blackburn, George M., and Sherman L. Ricards. "The Prostitutes and Gamblers of Virginia City, Nevada: 1870." *Pacific Historical Review* 48, no. 2 (1979): 239–58.

Browne, J. Ross. *A Peep at Washoe and Washoe Revisited.* First printed in 1860 and 1865. Reprint, Balboa Island, CA: Paisano Press, 1959.

Cain, Ella M. *The Story of Bodie*. San Francisco, CA: Fearon Publishing, 1956.

Chalmers, Claudine. *French San Francisco*. Charleston, SC: Arcadia Publishing, 2007.

Chung, Sue Fong. *In Pursuit of Gold: Chinese American Miners and Merchants in the American West*. Champaign: University of Illinois Press, 2011.

Clapp, Nicholas. *Virginia City: To Dance with the Devil*. San Diego, CA: Sunbelt Publications, 2016.

Clark, Walter Van Tilburg, ed. *The Journals of Alfred Doten: 1849–1903*. Reno: University of Nevada Press, 1973.

Clemens, Samuel L. [Mark Twain]. *Roughing It*. First printed in 1872. Reprint, Berkeley: University of California Press, 1993.

Clemens, Samuel L. [Mark Twain], and Charles Dudley Warner. *The Gilded Age: A Tale of Today*. Hartford, CT: American Publishing Company, 1873.

Crouch, Gregory. *The Bonanza King: John Mackay and the Battle Over the Greatest Riches in the American West*. New York: Scribner, 2018.

Daniels, Zeke. *The Life and Death of Julia C. Bulette: "Queen of the Red Lights," Virginia City, Nevada*. Virginia City, NV: Lamp Post Publishing, 1958.

Datin, Richard C. *Elegance on C Street: The Story of the International Hotel*. Las Vegas: Nevada Publications, 1986.

DeArment, Robert K. *Knights of the Green Cloth: The Saga of the Frontier Gamblers*. Norman: University of Oklahoma Press, 1982.

Dixon, Kelly J. *Boomtown Saloons: Archaeology and History in Virginia City*. Reno: University of Nevada Press, 2005.

Drabelle, Dennis. *Mile-High Fever: Silver Mines, Boom Towns, and High Living on the Comstock Lode*. New York: St. Martin's Press, 2009.

Drury, Wells. *An Editor on the Comstock Lode*. First printed in 1936. Reprint, Reno: University of Nevada Press, 1984.

Earl, Phillip I. "Veiling the Tiger: The Crusade Against Gambling, 1859–1910." *Nevada Historical Society Quarterly* 29, no. 3 (1985): 175–204.

Earl, Phillip I., ed. *Heroes, Badmen, and Honest Miners: Joe Goodman's Tales of the Comstock Lode*. Reno, NV: Great Basin Press, 1977.

Enss, Chris. *Wicked Women: Notorious, Mischievous, and Wayward Ladies of the Old West*. Helena, MT: TwoDot Publishing, 2015.

Falk, Bernard. *The Naked Lady: Life Story of Adah Menken (Mazeppa)*. First printed in 1934. Reprint, London: Hutchinson, 1952.

Francaviglia, Richard V. *Hard Places: Reading the Landscape of America's Historic Mining Districts*. Iowa City: University of Iowa Press, 1997.

Gentry, Curt. *The Madams of San Francisco*. New York: Doubleday, 1964.

Goldman, Marion S. *Gold Diggers and Silver Miners: Prostitution and Social Life on the Comstock Lode*. Ann Arbor: University of Michigan Press, 1981.

———. "Sexual Commerce on the Comstock Lode." *Nevada Historical Society Quarterly* 21, no. 2 (1978): 99–129.

Haile, C.C. *The Family Jules: The Life and Times of Julia C. Bulette*. San Francisco, CA: Haile House Publishers, 2011.

Hegne, Barbara. *Harlots, Hurdies & Spirited Women of Virginia City, Nevada*. Sparks, NV: Privately printed, 2001.

Highton, Jake. *Nevada Newspaper Days: A History of Journalism in the Silver State*. Stockton, CA: Heritage West Books, 1990.

Hinckle, Warren, and Fredric Hobbs. *The Richest Place on Earth: The Story of Virginia City, Nevada, and the Heyday of the Comstock Lode*. Boston, MA: Houghton Mifflin Company, 1978.

James, Ronald M. *The Roar and the Silence: A History of Virginia City and the Comstock Lode*. Reno: University of Nevada Press, 1998.

———. *Temples of Justice: County Courthouses of Nevada*. Reno: University of Nevada Press, 1994.

———. *Virginia City: Secrets of a Western Past*. Lincoln: University of Nebraska Press, 2012.

———. "Women of the Mining West: Virginia City Revisited." *Nevada Historical Society Quarterly* 36, no. 3 (1993): 153–77.

James, Ronald M., and Susan A. James. *A Short History of Virginia City*. Reno: University of Nevada Press, 2014.

———. *Virginia City and the Big Bonanza*. Charleston, SC: Arcadia Publishing, 2009.

James, Ronald M., and C. Elizabeth Raymond, eds. *Comstock Women: The Making of a Mining Community*. Reno: University of Nevada Press, 1998.

James, Ronald M., and Robert E. Stewart, eds. *The Gold Rush Letters of E. Allen Grosh & Hosea B. Grosh*. Reno: University of Nevada Press, 2012.

James, Susan A. "Queen of Tarts." *Nevada Magazine*, September–October 1984.

L'Amour, Louis. *Comstock Lode*. New York: Bantam Books, 1981.

Lewis, Oscar. *Sagebrush Casinos: The Story of Legal Gambling in Nevada*. New York: Doubleday, 1953.

———. *Silver Kings: The Lives and Times of Mackay, Fair, Flood, and O'Brien, Lords of the Nevada Comstock Lode*. New York: Alfred A. Knopf, 1947.

Lingenfelter, Richard E., and Karen Rix Gash. *The Newspapers of Nevada: A History & Bibliography 1854–1919*. Reno: University of Nevada Press, 1984.

Lord, Eliot. *Comstock Mining and Miners*. First printed in 1883. Reprint, San Diego, CA: Howell-North Books, 1959.

Lyman, George D. *Ralston's Ring: California Plunders the Comstock Lode*. New York: Charles Scribner's Sons, 1937.

———. *The Saga of the Comstock Lode: Boom Days in Virginia City*. New York: Charles Scribner's Sons, 1944.

Magnaghi, Russell M. "Virginia City's Chinese Community, 1860–1880." *Nevada Historical Society Quarterly* 24, no. 2 (1981): 130–57.

Makley, Michael J. *The Apprentice Twain: A Novel About Mark Twain's Raucous and Hilarious Time in Virginia City*. Woodfords, CA: Eastern Sierra Press, 1993.

———. *The Infamous King of the Comstock: William Sharon and the Gilded Age in the West*. Reno: University of Nevada Press, 2006.

———. *John Mackay: Silver King in the Gilded Age*. Reno: University of Nevada Press, 2009.

Mathews, Mary McNair. *Ten Years in Nevada or Life on the Pacific Coast*. First printed in 1880. Reprint, Lincoln: University of Nebraska Press, 1985.

McDonald, Douglas. *The Legend of Julia Bulette and the Red Light Ladies of Nevada*. Las Vegas: Nevada Publications, 1980.

———. *Virginia City and the Silver Region of the Comstock Lode*. Las Vegas: Nevada Publications, 1982.

Mires, Peter B. *Lake Tahoe's Rustic Architecture*. Charleston, SC: Arcadia Publishing, 2016.

———. *Lost Carson City*. Charleston, SC: The History Press, 2018.

Moody, Eric N., ed. *Western Carpetbagger: The Extraordinary Memoirs of "Senator" Thomas Fitch*. Reno: University of Nevada Press, 1978.

Moody, Eric N., and Robert A. Nylen. "Silver Trumps Beer: The Sad Story of the Comstock's First Brewery." *Nevada in the West* magazine, Spring 2011.

Paher, Stanley W. *Nevada Ghost Towns & Mining Camps*. Berkeley, CA: Howell-North Books, 1970.

Paul, Rodman W. *California Gold: The Beginning of Mining in the Far West*. Cambridge, MA: Harvard University Press, 1947.

Seagraves, Anne. *Soiled Doves: Prostitution in the Early West*. Hayden, ID: WesAnne Publications, 1994.

Shinn, Charles H. *The Story of the Mine as Illustrated by the Great Comstock Lode of Nevada*. First printed in 1896. Reprint, Reno: University of Nevada Press, 1980.

Smith, Grant H. *The History of the Comstock Lode*. Reno: Nevada Bureau of Mines and Geology, 1943.

Stapp, Cheryl Anne. *The Stagecoach in Northern California: Rough Rides, Gold Camps & Daring Drivers*. Charleston, SC: The History Press, 2014.

Stewart, William M. *Reminiscences of Senator William M. Stewart of Nevada*. New York: Neale Publishing Company, 1908.

Taylor, Troy. *Wicked New Orleans: The Dark Side of the Big Easy*. Charleston, SC: The History Press, 2010.

Thoene, Brock. *The Legend of Storey County: A Novel*. Nashville, TN: Thomas Nelson Publishers, 1995.

Waldorf, John Taylor. *A Kid on the Comstock: Reminiscences of a Virginia City Childhood*. Reno: University of Nevada Press, 1970.

Wheeler, Richard S. *Sun Mountain: A Comstock Novel*. New York: Forge, 1999.

Williams, George, III. *The Red-Light Ladies of Virginia City, Nevada*. Dayton, NV: Tree By The River Publishing, 1984.

———. *Rosa May: The Search for a Mining Camp Legend*. Dayton, NV: Tree By The River Publishing, 1986.

Wright, William [Dan De Quille]. *The Big Bonanza*. First printed in 1876. Reprint, Las Vegas: Nevada Publications, 1974.

Zanjani, Sally. *Devils Will Reign: How Nevada Began*. Reno: University of Nevada Press, 2006.

ABOUT THE AUTHOR

Peter B. Mires, a Vermont native, has been fascinated with the western Great Basin and Sierra Nevada for thirty years. He received his doctorate in historical geography from Louisiana State University in 1988 and subsequently taught at the University of Minnesota–Duluth and the University of Delaware. His publications include several books and more than fifty scholarly articles, book reviews and op-ed pieces. Dr. Mires is retired and lives in Carson City, and when he is not reading or writing, he may be found hiking the Tahoe Rim Trail or exploring the Nevada outback.